GRAPHING CALCULATORS
IN THE SCIENCE CLASSROOM

GLENCOE
McGraw-Hill

New York, New York   Columbus, Ohio   Woodland Hills, California   Peoria, Illinois

Technology Consultants

Christine A. Lucas
Mathematics Teacher
Whitefish Bay High School
Whitefish Bay, Wisconsin

Jill Baumer-Piña
Former Program Assistant
The Ohio State University
Columbus, Ohio

Other Titles in the Glencoe Science Professional Series

Alternate Assessment in the Science Classroom
Cooperative Learning in the Science Classroom
Performance Assessment in the Science Classroom

Copyright © 1999 by Glencoe/McGraw-Hill.

All rights reserved. Printed in the United States of America. Except as permitted under the United States Copyrights Act of 1976, no part of this publication may be reproduced or distributed in any form or by any means, or stored in a database or retrieval system, without prior written permission of the publisher.

Send all inquiries to:
Glencoe/McGraw-Hill
8787 Orion Place
Columbus, OH 43240

ISBN: 0-02-825487-2

11 12 13   045   09 08 07

GRAPHING CALCULATORS IN THE SCIENCE CLASSROOM

Table of Contents

Introduction

An Introduction to Graphing Calculators 1
Using Graphing Calculators in Cooperative
    Learning 5
Graphing Calculators and the
    Mathematics Curriculum 6
Graphing Calculator Capabilities 7
Getting to Know Your Graphing
    Calculator 8

Evaluating Mathematical Expressions 11

Graphing Skills

Mode and Range 12
Functions 14
Trace and Zoom 16
Systems of Equations 19
Inequalities 21
Systems of Inequalities 23
Rational Functions 25
Radical Functions 27
Quadratic Relations 28
Trigonometric Functions and Their
    Inverses 30
Exponential and Logarithmic Functions 32

Applications

Solving Equations in One Variable 34
Solving Quadratic Equations 35
Families of Graphs 37
Maxima, Minima, and Zeros of Functions 39
Solving Trigonometric Equations 41
Verifying Trigonometric Identities 42
Solving Exponential and Logarithmic
    Equations 43

Matrices

Entering Matrices 44
Determinants, Inverses, and Operations 46

Statistics

Statistical Computations 48
Histograms 51
Scatter Plots and Lines of Regression 54
Curve Fitting 56

Probability and Combinatorics 60

Using Programs..62
Plotting Points in a Relation.............................63
Solving a System of Linear Equations................63
Using the Quadratic Formula............................64
Using the Law of Cosines..................................65
Using Hero's Formula..65
Inner and Cross Products of Vectors.................66
Sums of a Series..67
Sums in Summation Notation...........................67
Graphical Iteration..68
Mandelbrot Set..68
Generating Random Numbers..........................69
Evaluating a Function.......................................69
Area Between Two Curves................................70
Mickey Mouse...71

Templates
Casio fx-7700GE..73
HP 38G...74
Sharp EL-9200C...75
TI-81..76
TI-82..77
TI-83..78
TI-92..79

Appendix: Menus......................................80

Index...82

GRAPHING CALCULATORS IN THE SCIENCE CLASSROOM

An Introduction to Graphing Calculators

The graphing calculator offers you much more flexibility in studying graphs than can be obtained by paper and pencil graphing. Within seconds you can graph an equation or a system of equations that could take you several minutes to sketch. The various functions on a graphing calculator can also help you to analyze the graph in a way not possible with traditional graphing techniques. For example, when graphing an equation such as $y = x^4 + 3x^3 + 2x^2 - x - 10$, no longer do you have to spend time calculating the long list of ordered pairs that give you points to sketch the curve. No longer do you have to use the tedious repeated calculations of the Location Principle to find the zeros of the function. Instead, you can concentrate on the attributes of the graph itself—For what values of x is y increasing? Where does the graph reach a maximum point or does it have several maxima? Does the graph intersect the x-axis? If so, how many times? How does the behavior of the graph relate to the equation of the graph? and so on.

It is important to understand that it is okay and many times necessary to solve problems with a calculator and that most of the time the calculator does not "find the answer" but merely helps to find appropriate solutions to problems. If you do not understand how to interpret the information the calculator provides, then it is of no use. It is still up to you to make connections with the technology and the mathematical concepts. The calculator simply saves time and effort and allows you to go deeper into mathematical concepts than you could in the past. It also opens the door to solving previously-unsolvable problems.

The calculator is not the solve-all instrument for mathematical problems, but a tool for completing the tedious tasks that used to take hours and lots of paper to achieve before you could get to the real meat of the problem. You should experiment with the calculator to find applications that are appropriate to the topic being studied.

The graphing calculator allows you to look at many new areas of mathematics that until now were restricted at certain levels because of their difficulty. While it may take time to feel comfortable with using graphing calculators and you may be just beginning to learn how to use them, it is important to keep trying and to keep learning. Knowing when and how to use a graphing calculator to solve problems will help you become a better problem solver and that, of course, is the ultimate goal.

In this guide to using graphing calculators in the science classroom, you will encounter keystroke instructions for graphing various types of equations, as well as mathematical computations. Graphing calculators are scientific calculators, as well as hand-held computers, thus eliminating the need for one calculator to graph and one to compute. There are many manufacturers of graphing calculators including Casio, Hewlett-Packard, Sharp, and Texas Instruments. While all calculators share some common characteristics, each differs in its complexity and capabilities to graph various types of functions.

In this guide, we will present keystrokes for Casio and Texas Instruments calculators. The material in this book is appropriate for both students and teachers. Some of the procedures and keying sequences found in this text may be helpful in interpreting the instruction guides for other calculators you may encounter.

To promote understanding of the sequencing of keystrokes provided in this booklet, read through the list of keystrokes first before entering them to make sure you understand the purpose and sequence. When solving a problem on your own for the first time, it may be wise to write out the keystrokes first before entering them into the calculator.

Casio Calculators

There are several different Casio graphing calculators. There is also more than one model available within each number series of calculator. This guide includes keying sequences for the Casio fx-7700GE calculator. It has a variety of capabilities that permit you to perform calculations and statistical analyses. It can graph equations in a rectangular coordinate system, as well as graph inequalities and parametric equations. In addition to real number calculations, the fx-7700GE can perform operations on matrices. The Casio fx-8700G is a more advanced version of the fx-7700G, appropriate for college-level mathematics and engineering. Each calculator has programming capabilities that you can study in detail by consulting the owner's manual that comes with the calculator.

Hewlett Packard Calculators

The Hewlett Packard family of graphing calculators includes the HP 38G, HP 48G, and HP 48GX. All of the Hewlett Packard models include pop-up menus, input forms, and a built-in infrared input/output port that lets you send and receive files without using a cable. The input forms provide a method to set up a problem by letting you fill in blanks. The HP 38G stores a history of calculations, allowing you to scroll back and copy a previous input or result. It is capable of showing an expression numerically, graphically, and symbolically; and the split-screen feature lets you choose which two screens you want to use for comparison. The HP 38G includes matrix operations and has the ability to graph polar equations. It does not have the ability to graph inequalities but it can shade and determine the area of a region between a line or a curve and the *x*-axis or another line or curve. The HP 38G is the only calculator with ApLets. These are notes, pictures, graphs, and custom-designed views combined into an electronic lesson that allows you to explore a problem. ApLets are available from Hewlett Packard on floppy disk, at their Internet site, and on their bulletin board. You can even create your own ApLets. The HP 48G operates very similarly to the HP 38G but has enhancements that include three-dimensional graphics, and built-in equations. The HP 48GX has four times more memory than the other two models and has two expansion ports so you can add more memory or customize it with plug-in application cards.

Sharp Calculators

The Sharp EL-9200C and EL-9300C graphing calculators have an equation editor feature that allows you to enter an expression exactly the way it appears in the textbook. Both models include menus from which you can select specialized modes. Matrix operations are included in the calculation mode, while the graph mode lets you graph functions using rectangular or parametric coordinates. A unique feature in the graph mode is the jump key. If you are in the rectangular coordinate mode, this feature lets you jump to an intersection point, minimum and maximum values, and x- and y-intercepts. All the commands needed in the program mode are in the menus or on the keyboard. The statistics graph mode lets you graph data entered in the statistics mode. There are six kinds of data graphs and six kinds of regression curves. The EL-9300C operates very similarly to the EL-9200C but has enhanced features including a communications port, four times as much memory, and an equation solver function. The solver mode provides three methods to solve for different variables in equations.

Texas Instruments Calculators

The Texas Instruments family of graphing calculators includes the TI-80, TI-81, TI-82, TI-83, TI-85, and TI-92. This guide includes sequences for the TI-81, and TI-82/83 models. All of the Texas Instruments models allow you to graph equations and inequalities in a rectangular coordinate system, as well as to graph parametric equations. The higher the model number, the more sophisticated the programming capabilities of the calculator. These and the matrix feature of the TI-81 are expanded in the TI-82/83 to include list operations, sequences, tables, and more. The TI-85 has additional features that are specially suited to college-level mathematics and engineering. The TI-92 has greatly expanded memory, and offers symbolic manipulation, three-dimensional graphing, and the ability to construct, measure, and manipulate geometric figures.

GRAPHING CALCULATORS IN THE SCIENCE CLASSROOM

Using Graphing Calculators in Cooperative Learning

Cooperation is part of the real world at all levels, whether it be among nations, with co-workers, with neighbors, with your community, or within your family. Individuals must develop skills and understandings of working in groups to be successful in today's world.

The graphing calculator is a tool that will allow students to work in groups, explore concepts, and come to conclusions about the "rules" of mathematics through their own understanding. Research has shown that discovery and internalization of this type is more deeply understood than the dissemination of information usually seen in a traditional lecture situation.

When students use a graphing calculator, they find that they too have a powerful tool for asking "What if...?" By encouraging students to explore with the calculator, you open an unlimited world of variety in viewing each function they graph. For example, when graphing a line with graph paper, they may anticipate the graph to look a certain way. However, with the graphing calculator, the appearance of the graph depends on the range values used in the viewing window. By changing the scale, students can make a graph appear more or less steep than it is on traditional square grid paper.

When students graph more than one function on a viewing screen, they can explore how the two graphs are related. For example, if two lines are graphed, you could ask "Are the lines parallel or not? How do you know? Could the lines be perpendicular? How do you know? Do the lines have any characteristics in common?" and so on.

The cooperative group becomes a field for questioning and exploring. Emphasis is placed on the discovery method. Because the calculator saves time and is usually more accurate than student-drawn sketches, the technical aspect of graphing is set aside so that the real mathematics behind the graph can be explored. That is, you are enabled with the power to teach *more* mathematics by removing the mechanical manipulation time previously required with paper and pencil.

In addition to graphing activities, the graphing calculator lets students explore computational patterns. When entering mathematical expressions into the graphing calculator, unlike other scientific calculators, the entire expression appears on the screen as well as the final result. The REPLAY feature on the calculator allows you to return to the original expression and alter one or more parts of the expression. In this way, students can explore patterns in numbers that lead to a formula.

The expression "two heads are better than one" seems appropriate when working in cooperative groups. With a graphing calculator and a little guidance, students can use their collective resources to discover the same excitement about mathematics and science that motivated the mathematicians and scientists of the past to bring us the concepts we study today.

You can learn more about using cooperative learning techniques in Glencoe's Cooperative Learning in the Science Classroom, another booklet in the Glencoe Science Professional Series.

Graphing Calculators and the Mathematics Curriculum

The graphing calculator skills you will develop in the following pages can be used in a variety of courses in the mathematics curriculum. The chart below lists some of those skills and the course(s) for which they may be appropriate. This list is not all inclusive, and many of the skills thought of as second-year algebra topics are now available to students in first-year algebra or middle school courses by the power of the calculator.

Mathematical Skills	Mathematical Operations				
	Middle School	Algebra 1	Geometry	Algebra 2	Advanced Mathematics
Evaluate numerical expressions	✓	✓	✓	✓	✓
Perform operations with fractions resulting in fractions (Casio fx-7700 only)	✓	✓	✓	✓	✓
Graph linear functions	✓	✓	✓	✓	✓
Graph quadratic functions	✓	✓	✓	✓	✓
Graph polynomial functions		✓	✓	✓	✓
Graph inequalities	✓	✓	✓	✓	✓
Graph trigonometric functions		✓	✓	✓	✓
Graph inverse trigonometric functions				✓	✓
Graph exponential functions				✓	✓
Graph logarithmic functions				✓	✓
Graph parametric equations					✓
Graph polar equations					✓
Perform operations with matrices		✓	✓	✓	✓
Plot points	✓	✓	✓	✓	✓
Connect points with segments	✓	✓	✓	✓	✓
Draw histograms (bar graphs)	✓	✓	✓	✓	✓
Graph scatter plots	✓	✓	✓	✓	✓
Statistical computations (mean, standard deviation, regressions, correlation coefficients)	✓	✓	✓	✓	✓
Find the number of permutations	✓	✓	✓	✓	✓
Find the number of combinations	✓	✓	✓	✓	✓
Convert degrees to radians and vice versa			✓	✓	✓
Convert polar coordinates to rectangular coordinates and vice versa				✓	✓

Graphing Calculator Capabilities

Capability	Casio fx-7700GE	HP 38G	Sharp EL-9200C	TI-81	TI-82/83	TI-92
Evaluate numerical expressions	✓	✓	✓	✓	✓	✓
Perform operations with fractions resulting in fractions	✓	✓	✓		✓	✓
Graph linear and quadratic functions	✓	✓	✓	✓	✓	✓
Graph other polynomial functions	✓	✓	✓	✓	✓	✓
Graph inequalities	✓	✓	✓	✓	✓	✓
Graph trigonometric functions and inverses	✓	✓	✓	✓	✓	✓
Graph exponential and logarithmic functions	✓	✓	✓	✓	✓	✓
Graph parametric equations	✓	✓	✓	✓	✓	✓
Graph polar equations	✓	✓	✓	✓	✓	✓
Perform operations with matrices	✓	✓	✓	✓	✓	✓
Plot points, draw segments	✓		✓	✓	✓	✓
Graph histograms and scatter plots	✓	✓	✓	✓	✓	✓
Perform statistical computations	✓	✓	✓	✓	✓	✓
Calculate combinations and permutations	✓	✓	✓	✓	✓	✓
Convert degrees to radians, vice versa	✓	✓		✓	✓	✓
Convert polar coordinates to rectangular coordinates, vice versa	✓		✓	✓	✓	✓
Replay function	✓	✓	✓	✓	✓	✓
Linear Regression	✓	✓	✓	✓	✓	✓
Zooming in or out on image	✓	✓	✓	✓	✓	✓
Tracing to find the coordinates of a point	✓	✓	✓	✓	✓	✓
Programmable	✓	✓	✓	✓	✓	✓
Table of function values		✓			✓	✓
Draw, measure, transform geometric figures						✓
Three-dimensional drawing						✓
Symbolic manipulation						✓
Complex number calculations		✓	✓		✓ (TI-83)	✓
Advanced calculus operations		✓				✓

GRAPHING CALCULATORS IN THE SCIENCE CLASSROOM

Getting to Know Your Graphing Calculator

As with any new acquaintance, you need time to get to know your graphing calculator. Before beginning any specific task, look at the keyboard. Think of something you are used to seeing on your familiar scientific calculator and see if you can find it on your graphing calculator. Before delving into the manual, see if you can find a correlation to the expressions written above the keys and how to access them. Try to figure out what key is equivalent to = on your old calculator. Try various keys to see what happens. If you receive an error message of some sort, turn the calculator off and then on again. Questions will inevitably arise that you need special help in answering. When that happens, consult the calculator manual or a colleague.

It is very important that students also get to know the calculator. The first session you have with graphing calculators in the classroom should be a "play" period in which students explore the keys as described above. Let students work in pairs sharing a calculator. By working with a partner, students can share ideas about which key does what, and if they should get stuck, the problem-solving skills of two people working together will often be enough to overcome the difficulty.

In this section, we will explore some of the basic functions of the calculator and how to access menus on the Casio fx-7700GE and the TI calculators. Greater detail on how to use the menus for specific tasks are discussed later in this booklet.

How do I turn the calculator on?
Casio: Press [AC].
TI: Press [ON].

How do I turn the calculator off?
Casio: Press [SHIFT] [OFF] (located above [AC]).
TI: Press [2nd] [OFF] (located above [ON]).

All calculators have an automatic turnoff feature to prolong battery life. If the calculator is left on too long without being used, it automatically shuts itself off. If you press [AC] on the Casio calculator, the calculator will come on, but you lose whatever was in the text screen. If you press [ON] on a TI calculator, it will come on with the same screen image it had when it shut off.

How do I change the contrast so that I can see the screen better?
Casio: [MENU] [A] and ▶ repeatedly (to darken) or ◀ (to lighten).

TI: Press [2nd] and hold down ▲ to darken, or press [2nd] and hold down ▼ to lighten. A cursor appears in the upper right-hand corner with a number from 1–9 to represent the contrast. The higher the number, the darker the screen. If you wish to change the contrast further after the first adjustment, you must press [2nd] again before using either arrow key again.

If you turn your calculator on and the screen is blank or black, you may need to use the contrast adjustment to achieve the correct viewing setting. If you must increasingly darken your screen to read the display, it may be time to change the batteries.

How do I use the functions written above the keys?
Casio: Pressing [SHIFT] accesses the functions printed in yellow above left of the key. Pressing [ALPHA] accesses the functions printed in red above right of the key.

TI: Pressing [2nd] accesses the functions printed in blue above left of the key. Pressing [ALPHA] accesses functions printed in gray above right of the key.

In the keystroke sequences in this booklet, these functions are shown using the appropriate access key and the function name rather than the actual key pressed.

How do I clear what's on the screen?

Casio: Press [AC] to completely clear the displayed formulas, numeric values, and texts. Use the Cls (ClearScreen) function to clear graphs from the screen. Press [SHIFT] [F5] [EXE].

TI: Press [CLEAR] to completely clear the displayed formulas, numeric values, or text. Clear graphs by pressing [Y=] [CLEAR] [ENTER] for each line that has an equation. To clear any images created with the DRAW menu, press [2nd] [PRGM], which accesses the DRAW menu. Then select ClrDraw and press [ENTER].

How do I get out of a menu?

Casio: Pressing the [EXIT] key returns you to the home screen.

TI: The "QUIT" function lets you exit any menu. On the TI-81, QUIT is accessed by pressing [2nd] [CLEAR]. On the TI-82/83, QUIT is [2nd] [MODE].

Where do I find the [=] key on my calculator?

The graphing calculator is actually a small computer. The [=] key is replaced by [EXE] on Casio calculators and by [ENTER] on TI calculators.

How do I enter variables in an equation like $y = x + 2$?

When graphing an equation like the one above, it is not necessary to literally enter the letter Y and the equals sign. The X is entered differently depending on the calculator you have. For more information on how to enter a function in order to graph it, see pages 14–15.

Do I have to start over if I make a mistake in entering an expression?

The answer is no. If you make a mistake while entering the expression, you can use the left and right arrow keys to go back through the expression and correct your mistake. If the mistake is a wrong number or operation, you can simply "type over" the error with the correct number or operation. If you left out something, move the cursor to the point where you want to insert the information and use the [INS] key to insert the new information.

Casio: [DEL]
TI-81: [INS]
TI-82/83: [2nd] [DEL]

Likewise, you can move the cursor and use [DEL] to remove any unnecessary information.

When I use the square root key, do I press the function key before or after entering the number?

The graphing calculator, unlike some scientific calculators, works like a mathematical sentence writer. In fact, you see the sentence on the screen as you create it. If you want to find $\sqrt{4356}$, press the keys in the order you would read it.

Casio: Press [SHIFT] [√] and then enter the number, 4356. To calculate the result, press [EXE].

TI: Press [2nd] [x^2] to access the square root sign. Then enter the number. To calculate, press [ENTER].

Is the order of entering a trigonometric function similar to the way we enter a square root sign?

The answer is yes. With many scientific calculators, you must enter the angle being evaluated and then press the appropriate key. With a graphing calculator, you should enter the function first and then the angle measure.

Is there a pi key on my calculator?

The answer is yes. On the Casio calculator, π is entered by pressing [SHIFT] [EXP]. On the TI calculators, it is the second function of [^].

More information on how to access other function keys is found in the instructions for the specific mathematical skills for which they are used. *See Index on page 82.*

How do I know what's on each menu?

The TI calculators and Casio fx-7700GE have many functions that are accessed by using menus (lists of options) and making selections. Sometimes you may know what function you want to use, but you have no idea where to find it. In the Appendix on pages 80–81, you will find many of the menus that are available on each calculator, how to access them, and what each item on the menu means. In future pages of this booklet, we will show the actual keying sequence to access items in menus which are used for specific mathematical tasks.

How do I use the TI menus?

Several keys on the TI calculators access menus. These menus are discussed in greater detail as we use them in this booklet. Page 81 also lists many of the menus in greater detail.

Most of the menu keys actually access several menus. Each of these is shown at the top of the screen and can be accessed by using ▶ or ◀ to highlight the menu you wish to use. The items in each menu can be accessed by pressing the number of the item or by using ▲ or ▼ to highlight the item and then pressing ENTER.

Many of the menus on the TI-81 and TI-82 are the same. The TI-82 and TI-83 have more menus and thus more features.

How do I use the menus on the Casio fx-7700G?

The menus on the Casio fx-7700G operate much differently than those on TI calculators. Menus can be accessed using second function keys. Selections from menus are made by using the top row of keys (F1 through F6).

For example, when you press SHIFT, six rectangles appear at the bottom of the screen. Each of these rectangles correspond to the F1 through F6 keys respectively. Not all menus have six selections. When only four rectangles appear, then these correspond to keys F1 through F4.

Regardless of how many rectangles appear, the rectangles do not appear directly over the keys to which they correspond. You must count which rectangle you want to use and press the corresponding F key. For example, if you want to use the function defined in the fourth rectangle, F4 is the key you press to access that function.

All of the Casio functions are abbreviated by four or less symbols. It may be helpful to make a list of what each symbol represents until you become familiar with the menus. Page 80 of the Appendix gives further details on some of the more commonly-used menu items and their functions.

Other menus appear in specialized modes, such as SD for statistical data, REG for regression calculations, and MATRIX for matrix entry and operations. As with other menus, rectangles appear at the bottom of the screen that correspond to the F1 through F6 keys.

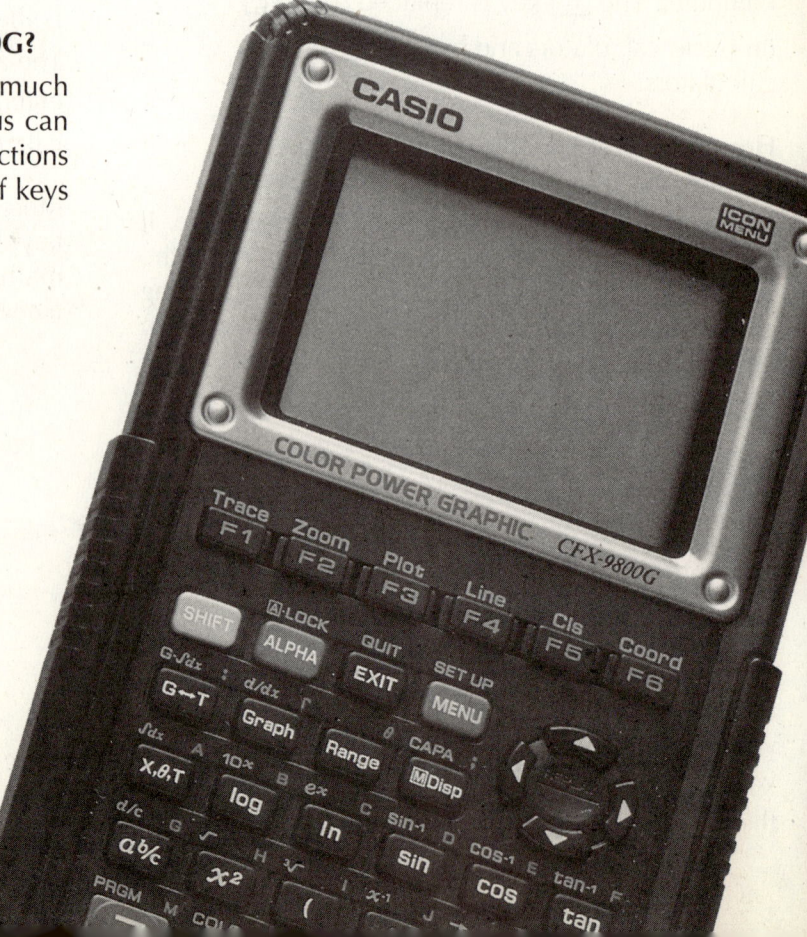

Evaluating Mathematical Expressions

● Casio fx-7700GE   ● TI-81   ● TI-82/83

All graphing calculators observe the order of operations when evaluating a mathematical expression. The calculators also have parentheses that are used in the same way as in writing to group terms in an expression or to clarify the meaning of the expression.

When you enter an expression in a graphing calculator, the entire expression appears as you enter it. On TI calculators, the multiplication and division signs do not appear as they do on the keys. Instead the calculator displays symbols used in computer language. That is, * means multiplication, and / means division.

If you make a mistake, you can use the arrow keys to go back and correct your error by typing over, by using the [INS] (insert) key, or by using the [DEL] (delete) key.

1 Evaluate $\frac{2 + 3^2 - (-6)(-8)}{-4}$.

You must use parentheses to group the terms in the numerator.

Casio: [(] 2 [+] 3 [x²] [−] [(−)] 6 [×] [(−)] 8 [)] [÷] [(−)] 4 [EXE]

TI: [(] 2 [+] 3 [x²] [−] [(−)] 6 [×] [(−)] 8 [)] [÷] [(−)] 4 [ENTER]

The result is 9.25.

Note that the negative sign is entered before the number and that its key, [(−)], is different from the subtraction key [−].

You can also use parentheses to denote multiplication. Thus, (−6)(−8) can be entered that way on the calculator without using a multiplication symbol.

REPLAY If you get an error message or discover that you entered the expression incorrectly, you can use the REPLAY feature to correct your error and re-evaluate without re-entering the expression.

Casio: Press [→] or [←]. The answer disappears and the cursor goes to the beginning or end of the expression, respectively. Use the arrow keys to move to the location of the correction. Then type over, use [SHIFT] [INS], or use [DEL] to make the correction. Then press [EXE] to evaluate. You do not have to move the cursor to the end.

TI: On the TI-81 press [▲]. On the TI-82/83, press [2nd] [ENTRY]. The expression is redisplayed below the previous evaluation with the cursor at the end. Move the cursor using the arrows and make your changes. Then press [ENTER] to evaluate.

The REPLAY feature is very handy for evaluating polynomial expressions of high degree, such as $4x^4 - 5x^3 + 3x^2 - 45$, for varying values of x.

2 Evaluate $3x - 6$ for $x = 3, -3, 4,$ and 6.

Evaluate the expression for $x = 3$. Record the result. Use the REPLAY feature to change 3 to −3. Evaluate again. Repeat changing −3 to 4, and so on. If you use parentheses around the number representing x, it makes it easier to find the place to substitute when using the REPLAY feature.

Example: 3 [(] 3 [)] [−] 6

Mode and Range

- Casio fx-7700GE
- TI-81
- TI-82/83

MODE Each of the calculators has a [MODE] key. However, the type of mode and the way in which you select the mode is slightly different for each calculator. In future activities in this booklet, we will indicate when you need to change modes and what mode(s) to use.

Casio fx-7000GE: Pressing [MODE] once accesses the first menu screen shown below. Pressing [MODE] again accesses the second screen. To make a selection on either screen, press the key of the number or operation preceding your choice. *You can also get to the second MODE screen by pressing [SHIFT] [MODE].*

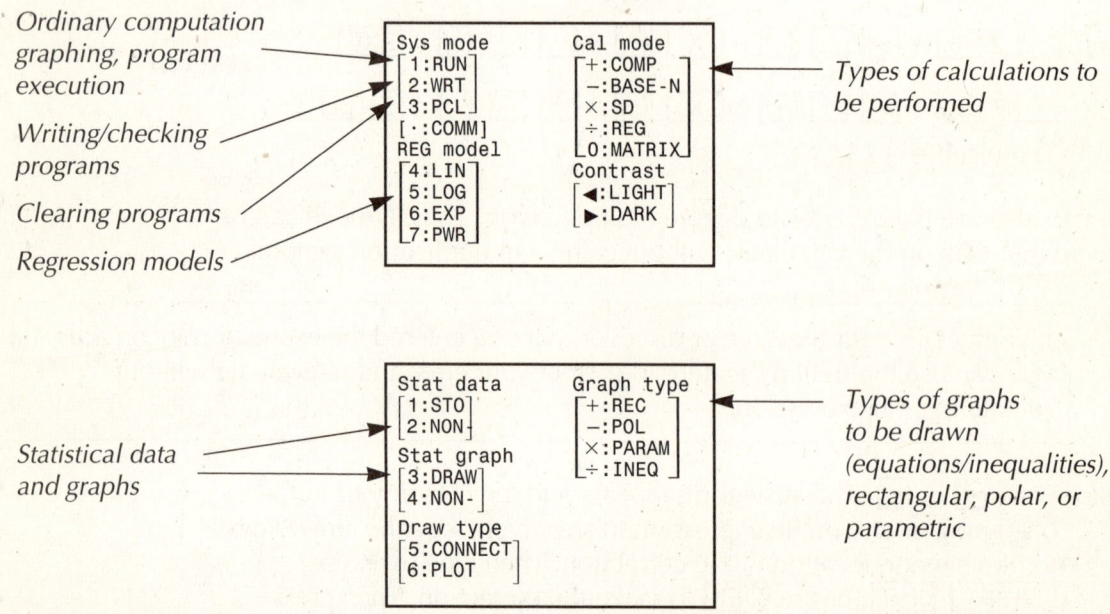

Ordinary computation graphing, program execution

Writing/checking programs

Clearing programs

Regression models

Types of calculations to be performed

Statistical data and graphs

Types of graphs to be drawn (equations/inequalities), rectangular, polar, or parametric

Notice the Draw type items at the lower left of the second screen. If you select 6:PLOT, individual points whose coordinates the calculator has computed will be shown on the graphing screen. If you select 5:CONNECT, then the calculator will plot the points and connect them.

TI: When you press [MODE], the mode screen appears. The settings that are highlighted with a gray tint represent the setting currently in use. You can change these settings by using the arrow keys to move the tint block and pressing [ENTER] to make your choice.

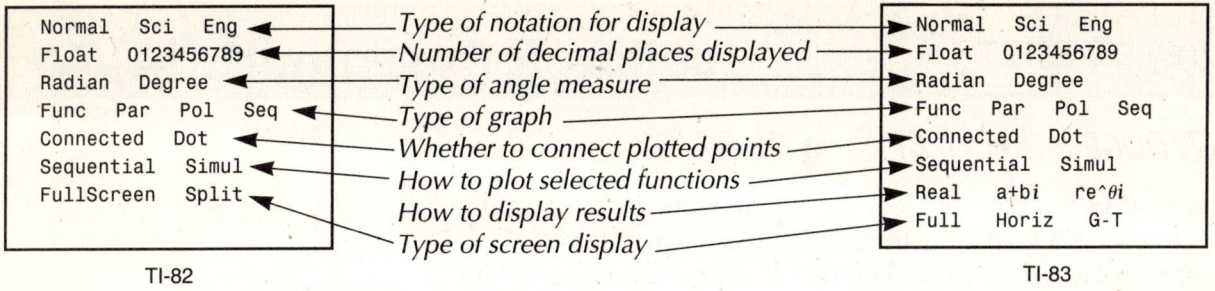

RANGE or WINDOW

Use the range feature to set the parameters for the viewing window, including not only the range for each axis but also the value of each tick mark on the graph.

On the TI-82/83, the RANGE *key is replaced by the* WINDOW *key.*

The range feature allows you to adjust how much of the graph you wish to view. The notation [−5, 5] by [−6, 6] means a viewing window in which the values along the *x*-axis go from −5 to 5 and the values along the *y*-axis go from −6 to 6. For all of these calculators, the range is set in a similar manner. When you press RANGE, a list of values appears. **Xmin** and **Xmax** mean the minimum and maximum values on the horizontal scale. **Xscl** represents how many units you wish each tick mark on the axis to represent. Likewise, **Ymin, Ymax,** and **Yscl** represent similar values along the vertical axis. To change a value from the list, use the arrow keys to scroll to the value you wish to change. Then type the new value and press EXE or ENTER. When you return to the graph screen, a new viewing window will be displayed and your graph will be redrawn. *For more information on graphing and viewing windows, see pages 12–13.*

```
WINDOW
Xmin = -5
Xmax = 5
Xscl = 1
Ymin = -6
Ymax = 6
Yscl = 1
Xres = 1
```
TI-83

The Casio fx-7700GE, TI-81, and TI-82/83 have parametric capabilities. When you choose parametric mode and access the range function, you will find that the list of parameters will also include entries for **Tmin, Tmax,** and **Tstep** (or **Tptch**). Enter these numbers according to your problem's parameters.

Each type of calculator has a default setting for range values. A default setting is one that is built into the calculator and is used when no other setting is specified. Many users prefer to begin with the default settings first and then adjust their viewing window as necessary.

Casio fx-7700GE: Range F1   Selects INIT range settings, that is, a viewing window of [− 4.7, 4.7] by [− 3.1, 3.1], with a scale factor of 1.

TI: ZOOM 6   Selects the standard viewing window, [−10, 10] by [−10, 10], with a scale factor of 1.

13

Functions

● Casio fx-7700GE   ● TI-81   ● TI-82/83

A graphing calculator is a powerful tool for studying functions. Any of the graphing calculators will graph functions, but the procedure for graphing is slightly different for each one. On any of the calculators, you must set an appropriate range before you can graph a function. A viewing window of $[-10, 10]$ by $[-10, 10]$ with a scale factor of 1 on both axes denotes the domain values $-10 \leq x \leq 10$ and the range values $-10 \leq y \leq 10$. The tick marks on both axes in this viewing window will be one unit apart. This is called the **standard viewing window.** The standard viewing window is a good place to start when graphing an unfamiliar function.

1 **Graph $y = 2x + 3$ in the standard viewing window.**

Before graphing, be sure that your calculator is in the correct mode for graphing functions on rectangular coordinates.

Casio fx-7700GE: [MENU] 1 [SHIFT] [SET UP] [F1] [EXIT]   *Sets COMP mode and rectangular coordinates.*

TI: Press the [MODE] key. If "Function" and "Rect" are not highlighted, use the arrow and [ENTER] keys to highlight them. Press [2nd] [QUIT] to return to the home screen.

Now graph the function.

Casio fx-7700GE: [Graph] 2 [X,θ,T] [+] 3 [EXE]

TI-81:   [Y=] 2 [X|T] [+] 3 [GRAPH]

TI-82/83: [Y=] 2 [X,T,θ] [+] 3 [GRAPH]

On the TI-82/83, x is entered using the [X,T,θ] key.

Unless you are going to graph two or more functions on the same screen, you will need to clear the currently graphed function (if any) before you graph another function. To do this on the Casio, press [SHIFT] [Cls] [EXE]. Changing the range before entering a new function to be graphed on the Casio calculator will also clear the graphics screen. To clear the graphics screen on a TI, press [Y=] and use the arrow and [CLEAR] keys to clear any equations from the Y = list.

When the equation in Example 1 is graphed on the standard viewing window, it is a **complete graph.** A complete graph shows all of the important characteristics of the graph. For a linear function, these are the *x*- and *y*-intercepts. A complete graph for a function of higher degree includes the *x*- and *y*-intercepts, all maximum or minimum points, points of inflection, and the end behavior.

2 **Graph $y = -16x^2 + 11$ so that a complete graph is shown.**

First graph on a standard viewing window.

Casio fx-7700GE: [Graph] [(−)] 16 [X,θ,T] [x²] [+] 11 [EXE]

TI-81: [Y=] [(−)] 16 [X|T] [x²] [+] 11 [GRAPH]

TI-82/83: [Y=] [(−)] 16 [X,T,θ] [x²] [+] 11 [GRAPH]

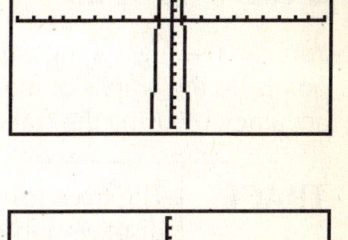

The standard viewing window does not show a complete graph. Try the range [−3, 3] by [−5, 15] with a scale factor of 1 for both axes. When you finish changing the range values, you do not need to reenter the equation. Press [Range] to exit the range menu and then press [EXE] to graph on a Casio calculator. Just press [GRAPH] on a TI calculator.

This range shows the complete graph of the function, including its intercepts, maximum point, and end behavior.

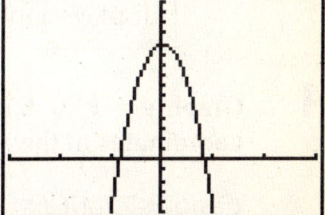

3 **Graph $y = x^4 - 3x^3 - 7x^2 - x + 2$ so that a complete graph is shown.**

Try the standard viewing window.

Casio fx-7700GE: [Graph] [X,θ,T] [^] 4 [−] 3 [X,θ,T] [^] 3 [−] 7 [X,θ,T] [x²] [−] [X,θ,T] [+] 2 [EXE]

TI-81: [Y=] [X|T] [^] 4 [−] 3 [X|T] [^] 3 [−] 7 [X|T] [x²] [−] [X|T] [+] 2 [GRAPH]

TI-82/83: [Y=] [X,T,θ] [^] 4 [−] 3 [X,T,θ] [^] 3 [−] 7 [X,T,θ] [x²] [−] [X,T,θ] [+] 2 [GRAPH]

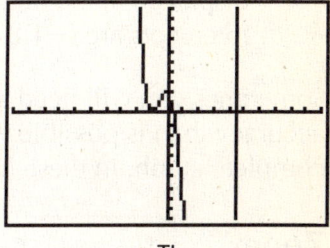
TI

The range [−4, 6] by [−70, 10] with scale factors of 1 for the x-axis and 10 for the y-axis shows a complete graph.

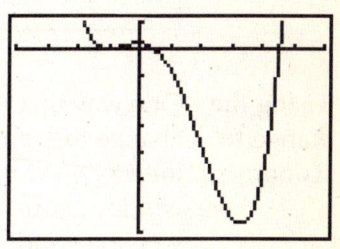

15

Trace and Zoom

- Casio fx-7700GE • TI-81 • TI-82/83

You can use a graphing calculator to find approximations of the coordinates of points on the graphs of functions. These coordinates can be found with great accuracy by using the **trace** and **zoom** features.

TRACE | The trace feature moves the cursor along the graph of a function and displays approximations of the coordinates of points on the graph.

1 Graph $y = x^3 + 6$ in the standard viewing window. Then trace to find the coordinates of the *x*- and *y*-intercepts.

Casio fx-7700GE: [Graph] [X,θ,T] [^] 3 [+] 6 [EXE]

TI-81: [Y=] [X|T] [^] 3 [+] 6 [GRAPH]

TI-82/83: [Y=] [X,T,θ] [^] 3 [+] 6 [GRAPH]

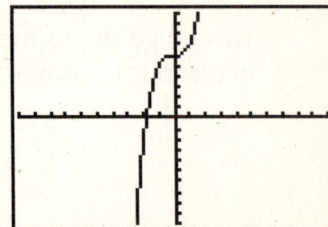

Now use the trace feature to determine the coordinates of the *x*- and *y*-intercepts. On the Casio calculator, press [SHIFT] [Trace] and on a TI, press [TRACE]. Then use the left and right arrow keys to move along the function to the intercepts. The coordinates of the point at the cursor are displayed at the bottom of the screen. The approximate coordinates of the intercepts are (−1.8, 0) and (0, 6).

Sometimes you will need to approximate the coordinates of a point with greater accuracy than is possible with tracing from a viewing window that shows a complete graph. In these cases, the zoom feature is very helpful.

Zoom | The zoom feature allows you to adjust the viewing window to show larger or smaller pieces of the graph of a function. Your calculator may offer you many methods for zooming in or out on a graph.

Using the Range to Zoom One way that you can zoom in or out on a graph is to manually change the range for the viewing window. For example, if you initially view the graph of $y = x^3 − 3x^2 + 7$ in the standard viewing window, you can see that the zero is between −2 and −1. Setting the viewing window to [−2, −1] by [−1, 1] with scale factors of 0.1 on both axes will allow you to make a closer approximation. You can then repeat this process as often as you like until you reach the desired accuracy or until you reach the limits of the calculator.

16

Box Zoom   Another method of zooming in that is available on the Casio fx-7700GE and the TI calculators is box zoom. With box zoom, the calculator prompts you to use the arrow keys to position the cursor at two opposite corners of a box to make a new viewing window. When you press the [EXE] or [ENTER] key, the calculator redraws the graph of the function in the range that you specified with the box. Use the following steps to use box zoom to zoom in on a part of the graph of a function displayed on the graphics window.

1. Press [SHIFT] [Zoom] on a Casio fx-7700GE or [ZOOM] on a TI calculator. Select Box by pressing [F1] or 1.

2. The graphics screen will appear with a cursor blinking in the center. Use the arrow keys to move the cursor to one corner of the box you want to define. Press [EXE] on the Casio fx-7700GE or [ENTER] on a TI calculator.

3. Move the cursor to the opposite corner of the box you want to define. Notice that as you move the cursor, the sides of the box change. Press [EXE] or [ENTER] and the calculator will redraw the graph in the new viewing window.

The location, size, and shape of the zoom box will usually change the appearance of a graph in a significant way. The *x*-coordinates for points on the vertical sides of a zoom box and the *y*-coordinates of the horizontal sides will automatically be made new Xmin, Xmax and Ymin, Ymax settings for the viewing window once you zoom to that box.

Note: If you change your mind about zooming into a box before you actually zoom into it, press [SHIFT] on the Casio calculator. If you are using a TI calculator, press any menu key to access a menu, [GRAPH] to return to the graphics screen, or [2nd] [QUIT] to return to the home screen.

If you attempt to locate the second corner of your box horizontally or vertically with the first corner, no box is formed for the next viewing window. In this case, the Casio fx-7700GE will not redraw the graph. It will wait for you to move the cursor to form a box and press [EXE] for the graph to be redrawn. If you locate the second corner of a box horizontally or vertically aligned with the first on a TI calculator, you will receive an error message. You will have to quit and then reaccess the box feature through the zoom menu to complete the zoom in process.

Zoom In and Zoom Out by Factors

A third method of zooming in and out, which uses factors, is available on each graphing calculator. With zooming by factors, the calculator will enlarge or reduce the graph around a chosen center point by a factor or factors that you choose. On the Casio fx-7700GE and the TI calculators, you can choose different factors for the two axes. For example, if you start with a standard viewing window and choose 1.5 for the x-factor and 2 for the y-factor and zoom in at the origin, the space occupied by 1.5 units on the x-axis or 2 units on the y-axis will be occupied by 1 unit on the new graph. Thus, the range for the new graph will be $[-6.67, 6.67]$ by $[-5, 5]$. Use the following steps to use factors to zoom in or out on a graph that is displayed on the graphics screen.

Casio fx-7700GE and TI: You may choose different factors for the x- and y-axes when you zoom in or out on the Casio fx-7700GE and the TI calculators. Use the following steps to choose the factors and zoom in or out.

1. Choose the factors by pressing [SHIFT] [ZOOM] [F2] on a Casio fx-7700GE or [ZOOM] 4 on a TI. Enter the factors and press [EXE] or [ENTER]. On the TI-82/83, press [ZOOM] [▶] 4 to access the screen for setting the zoom factors.

2. To zoom in or out on a Casio fx-7700GE, if you wish to zoom in around a point other than the center of the screen, use the trace function to move the cursor to the point. Then press [SHIFT] [Zoom] [F3] or [SHIFT] [Zoom] [F4].

   To zoom in or out on a TI, press [ZOOM] 2 or [ZOOM] 3. The graphics screen will appear with a blinking cursor at the center. Use the arrow keys to move the cursor to the point that you want to be the center of the zoom and press [ENTER]. You do not need to press [ZOOM] again to zoom in or out by the same factor. Use the arrow keys to move the cursor to the new center and press [ENTER].

> **Note:** The standard viewing window on the Casio fx-7700GE is a "friendly" window. If you graph a function on that window and then trace along the graph, the x-coordinates change by 0.1 with each tap of the [▶] and [◀] keys.
>
> This is not the case on the TI calculators. When you use the standard viewing window, the x-coordinates are "messy" decimals. You can obtain a friendly window by using a $[-4.7, 4.8]$ by $[-3.1, 3.2]$ setting on the TI-81. On the TI-82/83, use $[-4.7, 4.7]$ by $[-3.1, 3.1]$.

Systems of Equations

● *Casio fx-7700GE*   ● *TI-81*   ● *TI-82/83*

You can use a graphing calculator to graph and solve systems of equations since several equations can be graphed on the screen at one time. Graph the related functions for the system. Then use the trace and zoom features to approximate the solutions.

1 **Graph the system of equations $y = 3.4x + 2.1$ and $y = -5.1x + 8.3$ in the standard viewing window. Then determine the coordinates of the intersection point(s).**

Make sure your calculator is in the correct mode. If you are using a TI calculator, clear all of the equations from the Y = list first. If you are using a TI-82, you may have to turn off statistical plots by pressing [2nd] [STAT PLOT] 4 [ENTER].

Using the colon on the Casio calculators allows you to draw more than one graph at one time.

Casio fx-7700GE: [Graph] 3.4 [X,θ,T] [+] 2.1 [ALPHA] [:]
[Graph] [(−)] 5.1 [X,θ,T] [+] 8.3 [EXE]

TI-81: [Y=] 3.4 [X|T] [+] 2.1 [ENTER] [(−)] 5.1 [X|T] [+] 8.3 [GRAPH]

TI-82/83: [Y=] 3.4 [X,T,θ] [+] 2.1 [ENTER] [(−)] 5.1 [X,T,θ] [+] 8.3 [GRAPH]

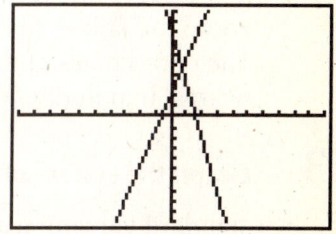

Now use the trace function to determine the coordinates of the intersection point. On the Casio calculators, press [SHIFT] [Trace] and on the TI calculators, press [TRACE]. Then use the left and right arrow keys to move along the graph to the intersection point. The Casio fx-7700GE and the TI calculators allow you to move from one function to another by pressing the up and down arrow keys.

Use the box zoom or zoom in by factors to pinpoint the intersection point. Repeatedly zooming and tracing allows you to find accurate approximations for the coordinates of the point of intersection. The coordinates of the point of intersection of $y = 3.4x + 2.1$ and $y = -5.1x + 8.3$ are (0.73, 4.58) rounded to the nearest hundredth.

> **Note:** The TI-82 and TI-83 have a special function on the CALC menu that will identify the point of intersection of two graphs. When "5: intersect" is selected from the CALC menu, a prompt saying "First curve?" appears. Move the cursor using [▲] or [▼] to select the first function. Then use [▶] or [◀] to move the cursor close to the point of intersection. When you are as close as you can get, press [ENTER]. Use the same procedure to answer the "Second curve?" prompt, except this time, press [ENTER] twice. The cursor automatically moves to the intersection, and the coordinates of that point are displayed at the bottom of the screen.

2 Graph the system of equations $y = -x^3 - 3x^2 + 9x$ and $y = -x^2 + 10x - 25$. Determine the coordinates of the intersection point(s).

Try graphing in the standard viewing window.

Casio fx-7700GE: [Graph] [(−)] [X,θ,T] [∧] 3 [−]
3 [X,θ,T] [x²] [+] 9 [X,θ,T]
[ALPHA] [:] [Graph] [(−)] [X,θ,T]
[x²] [+] 10 [X,θ,T] [−] 25 [EXE]

TI-81: [Y=] [(−)] [X|T] [∧] 3 [−] 3 [X|T] [x²] [+] 9 [X|T]
[ENTER] [(−)] [X|T] [x²] [+] 10 [X|T] [−] 25 [GRAPH]

TI-82/83: [Y=] [(−)] [X,T,θ] [∧] 3 [−] 3 [X,T,θ] [x²] [+] 9 [X,T,θ]
[ENTER] [(−)] [X,T,θ] [x²] [+] 10 [X,T,θ] [−] 25 [GRAPH]

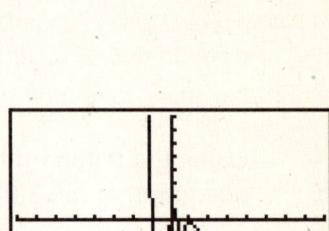

The standard viewing window does not show a complete graph. You must zoom out to view a complete graph so that you can determine how many solutions exist. Zooming out to a window of [−40, 40] by [−40, 40] shows that there is one solution to the system of equations. Now use the trace and zoom in features to determine the approximate coordinates of the solution. The coordinates of the intersection point are (2.30, −7.30) rounded to the nearest hundredth.

3 Graph the system of equations $y = \frac{2x+3}{x-1}$ and $y = \frac{3}{2}x - \frac{7}{2}$ in the standard viewing window. Determine the coordinates of the intersection point(s).

Casio fx-7700GE: [Graph] [(] 2 [X,θ,T] T [+] 3 [)] [÷]
[(] [X,θ,T] [−] 1 [)] [ALPHA]
[:] [Graph] 1.5 [X,θ,T] [−] 3.5 [EXE]

TI-81: [Y=] [(] 2 [X|T] [+] 3 [)] [÷] [(] [X|T] [−] 1 [)]
[ENTER] 1.5 [X|T] [−] 3.5 [GRAPH]

TI-82/83: [Y=] [(] 2 [X,T,θ] [+] 3 [)] [÷] [(] [X,T,θ] [−] 1 [)]
[ENTER] 1.5 [X,T,θ] [−] 3.5 [GRAPH]

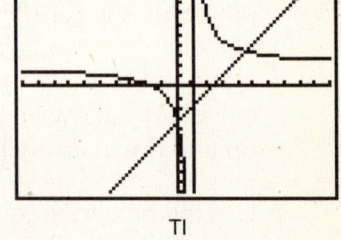

TI

The coordinates of the intersection points are (4.59, 3.39) and (0.07, −3.39) rounded to the nearest hundredth.

> **Note:** When a rational function has a vertical asymptote, your calculator may or may not display the asymptote. Whether it does or does not depends on the calculator you are using and on the viewing window.

Inequalities

- Casio fx-7700GE   • TI-81   • TI-82/83

The Casio fx-7700GE and TI calculators allow you to graph inequalities on the graphics screen. The procedures for graphing inequalities on a Casio fx-7700GE are similar to the procedures for graphing functions. Graphing inequalities on a TI requires using the "Shade(" command from the draw menu and entering a function for a lower boundary of the inequality and a function for the upper boundary. The calculator graphs both functions and then shades above the first function and below the second. Note that since this method draws on the graphics screen instead of graphing through the Y = list, editing these statements requires the methods you use to evaluate expressions instead of those you use to graph with the Y= list.

When graphing a linear inequality on a TI calculator, you can use the Ymin range value as the lower boundary if the inequality asks for "$y \leq$," since the points that satisfy the inequality are below the graph of the related equation. Use the Ymax range value as the upper boundary if the inequality asks for "$y \geq$," since the points that satisfy the inequality are above the graph of the related equation.

1   Graph $y \leq 3x + 4$ in the standard viewing window.

As with graphing functions, first clear the screen and set the range.

Casio fx-7700GE: Place the calculator in inequality mode. Then press [Graph] and choose the appropriate inequality symbol.

[MENU] 1 [SET UP] [F4] [EXIT]   Enter inequality (INEQ) mode.

[Graph] [F4] 3 [X,θ,T]   Choose the $\leq$ symbol and enter
[+] 4 [EXE]   the inequality.

TI: The inequality asks for "less than or equal to," so we will use Ymin as the lower boundary and the expression for the related equation $3x + 4$ as the upper boundary. The boundaries are entered as an ordered pair with the lower boundary first. Notice that by selecting "7" on the DRAW menu the shade feature appears with the left parenthesis in place. Be sure to enter the right parenthesis after the expressions.

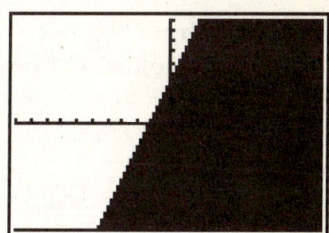

TI-81: [2nd] [DRAW] 7   Choose the shade option from the DRAW menu.

[VARS] [◄] 4 [ALPHA] [,] 3 [X|T]   Enter the lower and upper boundary
[+] 4 [)] [ENTER]   expressions and close with a right parenthesis. On the TI-82/83, it is not necessary to use the [ALPHA] key before [,].

TI-82/83: [2nd] [DRAW] 7 [VARS] 1 4 [,] 3 [X,T,θ] [+] 4 [)] [ENTER]

Since both the x- and the y-intercepts of the line $y = 3x + 4$ are within the standard viewing window, this is a complete graph of the inequality.

21

2 **Graph $y < x^3 - 6x^2 + 8$.**

Be sure to clear the graphics screen before graphing. Press [SHIFT] [Cls] [EXE] on the Casio fx-7700GE. Press [2nd] [DRAW] 1 [ENTER] on the TI since the draw menu was used instead of the Y= list to create the graph.

Try the standard viewing window.

Casio fx-7700GE: [Graph] [F2] [X,θ,T] [x^y] 3 [−] 6
[X,θ,T] [x²] [+] 8 [EXE]

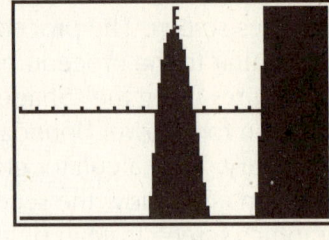

Note that the boundary is not included in the graph although it appears to be on the screen.

TI-81: Since the inequality symbol is <, the equation of the related function should be entered as the upper boundary in the "Shade" command. The Ymin value will be entered as the lower bound.

TI-82/83: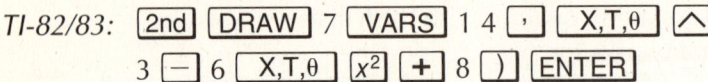

The standard viewing window does not show a complete graph of the inequality, since the minimum of the graph is not on the screen. Try the range [−10, 10] by [−30, 10] with a scale factor of 2 on the *x*-axis and 5 on the *y*-axis.

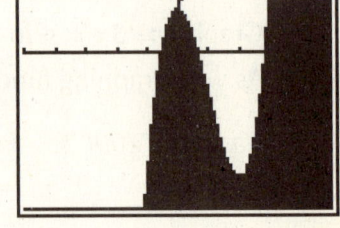

The command for graphing is the same on the Casio fx-7700GE, so after changing the range values press [Range] until you reach the text screen and then press [EXE] to regraph. For a TI, press [Range] and change the appropriate values. Then return to the text screen by pressing [2nd] [QUIT]. Press [ENTER] to redraw the graph.

3 **Graph $y > \log(6x + 3)$ in the viewing window [−3, 5] by [−3, 3] with scale factors of 1 on both axes.**

Casio fx-7700GE: [Graph] [F1] [log] [(] 6 [X,θ,T] [+] 3 [)] [EXE]

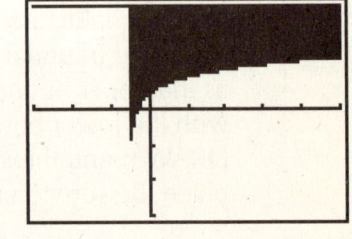

TI-81: [2nd] [DRAW] 7 [LOG] [(] 6 [XT] [+] 3 [)] [ALPHA] [,] 3 [)]
[ENTER]

TI-82/83: [2nd] [DRAW] 7 [LOG] [(] 6 [X,T,θ] [+] 3 [,] 3 [)]
[ENTER]

> **Note:** For the TI calculators, using the DRAW menu to generate graphs of inequalities makes the trace feature unavailable. Thus, you must use the free-moving cursor to explore these graphs. You can use features from the zoom menu, but since only graphs generated from the Y= list are automatically redrawn you must re-execute the shade command.

Systems of Inequalities

- *Casio fx-7700GE*   • *TI-81*   • *TI-82/83*

You can graph and solve a system of inequalities on a graphing calculator. When graphing on a Casio fx-7700GE, you will use the colon to separate the inequalities to be graphed. When graphing on a TI, you will use the shade command with the two inequalities entered as the upper and lower boundaries instead of a maximum or minimum value.

Since the TI graphs functions and shades above the first function entered and below the second function entered, the first step in solving a system is to decide which function to enter first as the lower boundary and which function to enter second as the upper boundary.

A "greater than or equal to" symbol indicates that values on and above the graph of the related function will satisfy the inequality. Similarly, a "less than or equal to" symbol indicates that values on and below the graph of the related function satisfy the inequality. Therefore, the related equation of the inequality with the sign $\geq$ will be entered first, and the related equation of the inequality with the sign $\leq$ will be entered second.

1 **Graph the system of inequalities $y < 3x - 5$ and $y \geq 2x^2 - 8$ in the standard viewing window.**

Be sure to clear the graphics screen before graphing. Press [SHIFT] [Cls] [EXE] on the Casio fx-7700GE, or clear the Y= list and press [2nd] [DRAW] 1 [ENTER] on the TI.

Casio fx-7700GE: [Graph] [F4] 3 [X,θ,T] [−] 5 [ALPHA] [:] [Graph] [F3] 2 [X,θ,T] [x²] [−] 8 [EXE]

TI-81: [2nd] [DRAW] 7 2 [X|T] [x²] [−] 8 [ALPHA] [,] 3 [X|T] [−] 5 [)] [ENTER]

TI-82/83: [2nd] [DRAW] 7 2 [X,T,θ] [x²] [−] 8 [,] 3 [X,T,θ] [−] 5 [)] [ENTER]

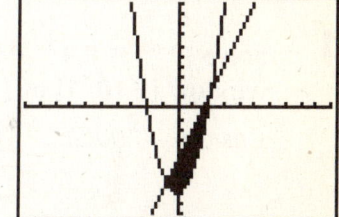

The points in the shaded area satisfy both $y \leq 3x - 5$ and $y \geq 2x^2 - 8$.

2 **Graph the system of inequalities $y \leq x^2$ and $y > \frac{4}{x}$ in the standard viewing window.**

Casio fx-7700GE: [Graph] [F4] [X,θ,T] [x²] [ALPHA] [:] [Graph] [F1] 4 [÷] [X,θ,T] [EXE]

TI-81: [2nd] [DRAW] 7 4 [÷] [X|T] [ALPHA] [,] [X|T] [x²] [)] [ENTER]

TI-82/83: [2nd] [DRAW] 7 4 [X,T,θ] [,] [X,T,θ] [x²] [)] [ENTER]

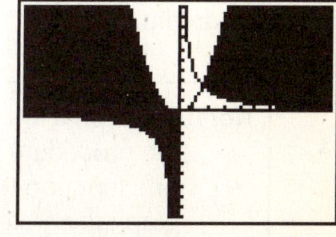

The graphing calculator can be used to solve inequalities by shading the area on the graph that makes the inequality true. To use this method, let each side of the inequality represent a separate inequality and graph the system of inequalities.

3 Solve $\sqrt{5x-3} \leq 3x - 8$ by graphing a system of inequalities.

Use the inequalities $\sqrt{5x-3} \leq y$ or $y \geq \sqrt{5x-3}$ and $y \leq 3x - 8$ as the system of inequalities to be graphed.

Casio fx-7700GE: [Graph] [F3] [√] [(] 5 [X,θ,T] [−] 3 [)] [ALPHA]
[:] [Graph] [F4] 3 [X,θ,T] [−] 8 [EXE]

TI-81: [2nd] [DRAW] 7 [2nd] [√] [(] 5 [XT] [−] 3 [)] [ALPHA] [,] 3
[XT] [−] 8 [)] [ENTER]

TI-82/83: [2nd] [DRAW] 7 [2nd] [√] [(] 5 [X,T,θ] [−] 3 [)] [,] 3
[X,T,θ] [−] 8 [)] [)] [ENTER]

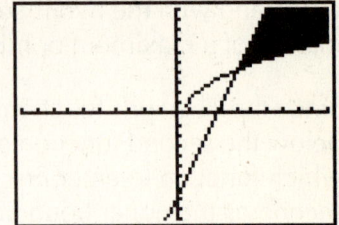

You can use the zoom feature to approximate a solution to the inequality. You may use the trace and zoom features of the Casio fx-7700GE on inequalities just as you do on functions. With a TI, the trace feature is not available since we used the draw menu to create the graph. You must use an arrow key to move the cursor to the edge of the shade and zoom in using the zoom menu. Then press [2nd] [QUIT] to return to the text screen and press [ENTER] to redraw the graph. The solution to the inequality is $x \geq 4.05$ to the nearest hundredth.

4 Solve $7^{x+4} \leq 0.1^{2x+8}$ by graphing a system of inequalities on the viewing window $[-10, 1]$ by $[-1, 3]$, with scale factor of 1 on each axis.

Casio fx-7700GE: [Graph] [F3] 7 [∧] [(] [X,θ,T] [+] 4 [)] [ALPHA]
[:] [Graph] [F4] .1 [∧] [(] 2 [X,θ,T] [+]
8 [)] [EXE]

TI-81: [2nd] [DRAW] 7 7 [∧] [(] [XT] [+] 4 [)] [ALPHA] [,] .1
[∧] [(] 2 [XT] [+] 8 [)] [)] [ENTER]

TI-82/83: [2nd] [DRAW] 7 7 [∧] [(] [X,T,θ] [+] 4 [)] [,] .1 [∧] [(] 2
[X,T,θ] [+] 8 [)] [)] [ENTER]

Zooming in shows that this inequality is true for $x \leq [-]4.00$ to the nearest hundredth.

> **Note:** To graph a system of inequalities such as $y > 2x - 1$ and $y > -x$ on the Casio fx-7700GE, use the procedure described in Example 1 on the preceding page. Since the TI calculators require one function to be the "bottom" function and the other to be the "top" function, you cannot graph the system $y > 2x - 1$ and $y > -x$ on a TI calculator by using the procedure described here.

Rational Functions

● *Casio fx-7700GE*   ● *TI-81*   ● *TI-82/83*

A rational function is one in which one polynomial is divided by another, or in mathematical terms, $f(x) = \frac{p(x)}{q(x)}$ where $q(x) \neq 0$. Rational functions usually have features that polynomial functions do not have, and the graphing calculator is a good tool to explore these graphs.

Some graphs of rational functions are discontinuous. The breaks in continuity can appear as asymptotes or as point discontinuities. A point discontinuity may not be visible in the first viewing window that you use to graph a rational function, so you may have to zoom in to see it or change the viewing window.

1 Graph $y = \frac{x^2 - 1}{x + 1}$. **Use a viewing window with scale factors of 1 for both axes.**

Since not all viewing windows allow you to see the point(s) of discontinuity, use the appropriate window for your calculator.

Casio window: [− 4.7, 4.7] by [− 3.1, 3.1]
TI-81 window: [− 4,7. 4.8] by [− 5, 5]
TI-82/83 window: [− 4.7, 4.7] by [− 3.2, 3.2]

Casio fx-7700GE: [Graph] [(] [X,θ,T] [x²] [−] 1 [)] [÷] [(] [X,θ,T] [+] 1 [)] [EXE]

TI-81: [Y=] [(] [XlT] [x²] [−] 1 [)] [÷] [(] [XlT] [+] 1 [)] [GRAPH]

TI-82/83: [Y=] [(] [X,T,θ] [x²] [−] 1 [)] [÷] [(] [X,T,θ] [+] 1 [)] [GRAPH]

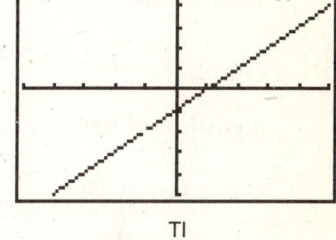
TI

The graph looks like a line with a break in continuity at $x = -1$.

Rational functions can also have asymptotes at values of x or y for which discontinuities occur. An asymptote can either be vertical or horizontal. Vertical asymptotes occur when the denominator equals zero. Horizontal asymptotes can be found by solving the equation for x and considering what number the function values are approaching as the absolute value of x becomes very large. Both asymptotes can be found graphically by using the zoom and trace features.

2 Graph $y = \frac{2x + 3}{x - 1}$. **Use the viewing window [−7, 7] by [−5, 10] with scale factors of 1 on both axes. Then find the equations of the vertical and horizontal asymptotes.**

Casio fx-7700GE: [Graph] [(] 2 [X,θ,T] [+] 3 [)] [÷] [(] [X,θ,T] [−] 1 [)] [EXE]

25

TI-81: [Y=] [(] 2 [X|T] [+] 3 [)] [÷] [(] [X|T] [−] 1 [)] [GRAPH]

TI-82/83: [Y=] [(] 2 [X,T,θ] [+] 3 [)] [÷] [(] [X,T,θ] [−] 1 [)] [GRAPH]

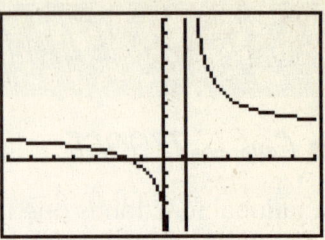

First find the vertical asymptote by tracing along the graph and observing the *x*-values near the discontinuity. As *y* increases, *x* approaches 1. On the TI calculators, use the integer function on the Zoom menu to adjust your viewing window. Press [ZOOM] 8. Then use the arrow keys to move the cursor to the origin and press [ENTER]. You can trace to a point where $x = 1$ and the calculator gives no *y*-value. This shows that the equation of the vertical asymptote is $x = 1$.

The asymptote may not appear in all viewing windows.

The horizontal asymptotes can be found by looking at the end behavior of the function. You can trace along the function to find that as *x* increases, *y* approaches 2. This can also be seen by graphing the function in a viewing window with large absolute values of *x*, such as [−1000, 1000] by [−5, 10], and tracing the function. The equation of the horizontal asymptote is $y = 2$.

In rational functions where the greatest exponent of the numerator is one greater than the greatest exponent of the denominator, the graph exhibits a slant asymptote. For example, $f(x) = \dfrac{x^2}{x - 6}$ has the line $y = x + 6$ as a slant asymptote and the line $x = 6$ as a vertical asymptote.

3 Graph $y = \dfrac{x^2 + 3x - 4}{x}$ in the standard viewing window. Determine the equation of the slant asymptote and graph it on the screen.

Casio fx-7700GE: [Graph] [(] [X,θ,T] [x²] [+] 3 [X,θ,T] [−] 4 [)] [÷] [X,θ,T] [EXE]

TI-81: [Y=] [(] [X|T] [x²] [+] 3 [X|T] [−] 4 [)] [÷] [X|T] [GRAPH]

TI-82/83: [Y=] [(] [X,T,θ] [x²] [+] 3 [X,T,θ] [−] 4 [)] [÷] [X,T,θ] [GRAPH]

The slant asymptote is found by writing the expression as a quotient.

$$\frac{x^2 + 3x - 4}{x} = x + 3 - \frac{4}{x}$$

As *x* approaches positive or negative infinity, $\dfrac{4}{x}$ approaches 0, which means that $x + 3 - \dfrac{4}{x}$ approaches $x + 3$. Therefore, the equation of the asymptote is $y = x + 3$. Use the keystrokes below to graph this equation.

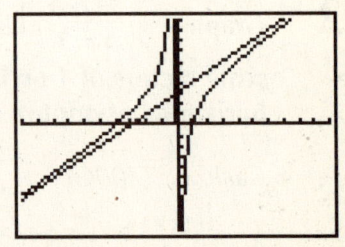

Use Y_2 on a TI calculator.

Casio fx-7700GE: [Graph] [X,θ,T] [+] 3 [EXE]

TI-81: [Y=] [X|T] [+] 3 [GRAPH]

TI-82/83: [Y=] [X,T,θ] [+] 3 [GRAPH]

Radical Functions

- Casio fx-7700GE   • TI-81   • TI-82/83

You can use a graphing calculator to graph various kinds of radical functions quickly and easily. To graph a radical function on the Casio graphing calculator, you can use the $\boxed{\sqrt{}}$, $\boxed{\sqrt[3]{}}$, or $\boxed{\sqrt[x]{}}$ keys. The TI calculators do not have a $\boxed{\sqrt[x]{}}$ key, although the TI-82/83 calculators do have $\boxed{\sqrt[x]{}}$ on the MATH menu that you access by pressing the $\boxed{\text{MATH}}$ key. On the TI-81, except for functions that use $\boxed{\sqrt{}}$ or $\boxed{\sqrt[3]{}}$, graphs of radical functions require that you use fractional exponents. If you have an equation of the form $y = \sqrt[n]{x}$, enter it into the calculator as $y = x^{\frac{1}{n}}$. For example, the equation $y = \sqrt[4]{x^3}$ can be graphed on a TI calculator by entering the equivalent equation of $y = x^{\frac{3}{4}}$ or $y = x^{0.75}$ using the $\boxed{\wedge}$ key. Be sure to use parentheses around fractions because without them, the calculator will interpret $x \boxed{\wedge} \frac{3}{4}$ to mean $x^3 \div 4$.

1 Graph $y = \sqrt{x - 3} + 1$ in the viewing window $[-1, 6]$ by $[-1, 6]$ with a scale factor of 1 on both axes.

Casio fx-7700GE: $\boxed{\text{Graph}}$ $\boxed{\text{SHIFT}}$ $\boxed{\sqrt{}}$ $\boxed{(}$ $\boxed{X,\theta,T}$ $\boxed{-}$ 3 $\boxed{)}$ $\boxed{+}$ 1 $\boxed{\text{EXE}}$

TI-81: $\boxed{Y=}$ $\boxed{\text{2nd}}$ $\boxed{\sqrt{}}$ $\boxed{(}$ $\boxed{X|T}$ $\boxed{-}$ 3 $\boxed{)}$ $\boxed{+}$ 1 $\boxed{\text{GRAPH}}$

TI-82/83: $\boxed{Y=}$ $\boxed{\text{2nd}}$ $\boxed{\sqrt{}}$ $\boxed{(}$ $\boxed{X,T,\theta}$ $\boxed{-}$ 3 $\boxed{)}$ $\boxed{+}$ 1 $\boxed{\text{GRAPH}}$

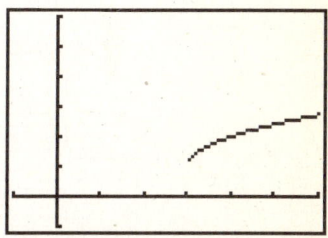

Why is there no graph when x is less than 3?

2 Graph the function $y = \sqrt[5]{3x + 4} - 4$ so that a complete graph is shown. Try the standard viewing window.

Casio fx-7700GE: $\boxed{\text{Graph}}$ 5 $\boxed{\text{SHIFT}}$ $\boxed{\sqrt[x]{}}$ $\boxed{(}$ 3 $\boxed{X,\theta,T}$ $\boxed{+}$ 4 $\boxed{)}$ $\boxed{-}$ 4 $\boxed{\text{EXE}}$

TI-81: $\boxed{Y=}$ $\boxed{(}$ 3 $\boxed{X|T}$ $\boxed{+}$ 4 $\boxed{)}$ $\boxed{\wedge}$ 0.2 $\boxed{-}$ 4 $\boxed{\text{GRAPH}}$

TI-82/83: $\boxed{Y=}$ $\boxed{(}$ 3 $\boxed{X,T,\theta}$ $\boxed{+}$ 4 $\boxed{)}$ $\boxed{\wedge}$ 0.2 $\boxed{-}$ 4 $\boxed{\text{GRAPH}}$
or $\boxed{Y=}$ 5 $\boxed{\text{MATH}}$ 5 $\boxed{(}$ 3 $\boxed{X,T,\theta}$ $\boxed{+}$ 4 $\boxed{)}$ $\boxed{-}$ 4 $\boxed{\text{GRAPH}}$

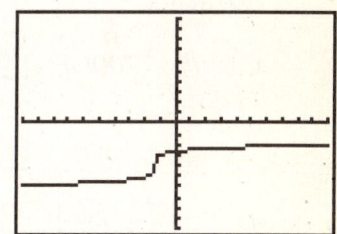

Since the end behavior and the point of inflection of the graph are shown, the standard viewing window shows a complete graph of the function.

Quadratic Relations

- *Casio fx-7700GE*   • *TI-81*   • *TI-82/83*

You can use a graphing calculator to graph relations; however you must do some algebra before you graph. A graphing calculator will only graph functions, so quadratic relations that are not functions must first be written as a combination of functions. For example, the equation of the parabola $x = y^2$ cannot be entered directly into the graphing calculator. We must solve the equation for y. In this case, you obtain $y = \pm\sqrt{x}$. To graph, you must enter the two functions $y = \sqrt{x}$ and $y = -\sqrt{x}$.

1 Graph the parabola whose equation is $x = y^2 + 5y + 22$ in the viewing window [0, 30] by [−10, 10] with scale factors of 1 on both axes.

First, solve the equation for y.

$$x = y^2 + 5y + 22$$
$$x + 6.25 = (y^2 + 5y + 6.25) + 22 \quad \text{Complete the square.}$$
$$x + 6.25 = (y + 2.5)^2 + 22 \quad \text{Simplify.}$$
$$x - 15.75 = (y + 2.5)^2 \quad \text{Subtract 22 from each side.}$$
$$\pm\sqrt{x - 15.75} = y + 2.5 \quad \text{Take the square root of each side.}$$
$$\pm\sqrt{x - 15.75} - 2.5 = y \quad \text{Subtract 2.5 from each side.}$$

Now enter the two equations $y = \sqrt{x - 15.75} - 2.5$ and $y = -\sqrt{x - 15.75} - 2.5$ into the graphing calculator. Since both of these equations are functions, they can be graphed on a graphing calculator.

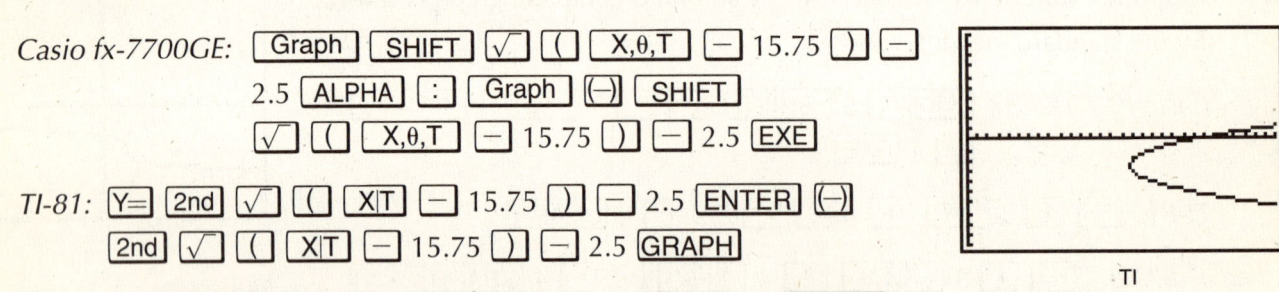

Casio fx-7700GE: [Graph] [SHIFT] [√] [(( ] [X,θ,T] [−] 15.75 [ )] [−] 2.5 [ALPHA] [:] [Graph] [(−)] [SHIFT] [√] [(( ] [X,θ,T] [−] 15.75 [ )] [−] 2.5 [EXE]

TI-81: [Y=] [2nd] [√] [(( ] [XǀT] [−] 15.75 [ )] [−] 2.5 [ENTER] [(−)] [2nd] [√] [(( ] [XǀT] [−] 15.75 [ )] [−] 2.5 [GRAPH]

TI-82/83: [Y=] [2nd] [√] [(( ] [X,T,θ] [−] 15.75 [ )] [−] 2.5 [ENTER] [(−)] [2nd] [√] [(( ] [X,T,θ] [−] 15.75 [ )] [−] 2.5 [GRAPH]

2 Graph the circle whose equation is $x^2 + y^2 = 16$.

Solve the equation for y.

$x^2 + y^2 = 16$
$\quad y^2 = 16 - x^2 \qquad$ Subtract x^2 from each side.
$\quad y = \pm \sqrt{16 - x^2} \qquad$ Take the square root of each side.

Use the standard viewing window.

Casio fx-7700GE: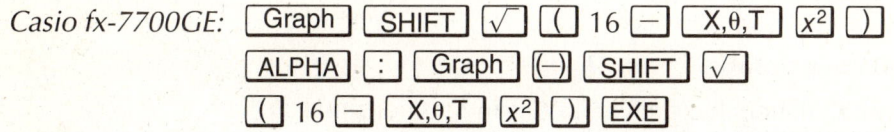

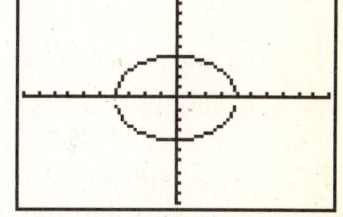

The Y-vars menu on the TI calculators allows you to use the name of a function as a variable in other expressions. In this case, we will define one of the two functions for graphing a circle as Y_1 and then define the second function as $-Y_1$.

TI-81: [Y=] [2nd] [√] [(] 16 [−] [X|T] [x²] [)] [ENTER] [(−)] [2nd] [Y-VARS] 1 [GRAPH]

TI-82/83: [Y=] [2nd] [√] [(] 16 [−] [X,T,θ] [x²] [)] [ENTER] [2nd] [(−)] [Y-VARS] 1 1 [GRAPH]

The graph appears to be an ellipse even though it is actually a circle. Since the viewing window is not scaled so that one unit on the *x*- and *y*-axes are displayed as an equal length, the graph is distorted. Thus, the scales must be adjusted so that the units on the *x*- and *y*-axes are equal in length.

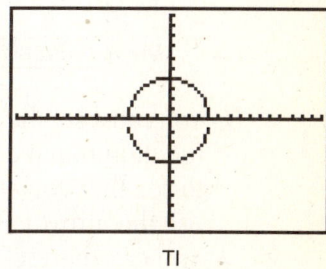

TI

You can make the graph square on the TI calculators by pressing [ZOOM] 5. On the Casio fx-7700GE, press [Range] [F1] [Range] [Range] [EXE]. The range produced on the Casio calculators is square, but in this case the range does not allow you to see a complete graph. We must use a multiple of this "default range" to view a complete square graph. Use [−9.4, 9.4] by [−6.2, 6.2] with a scale factor of 1 for both axes. This viewing window gives a complete graph of the functions and the graph appears as a circle.

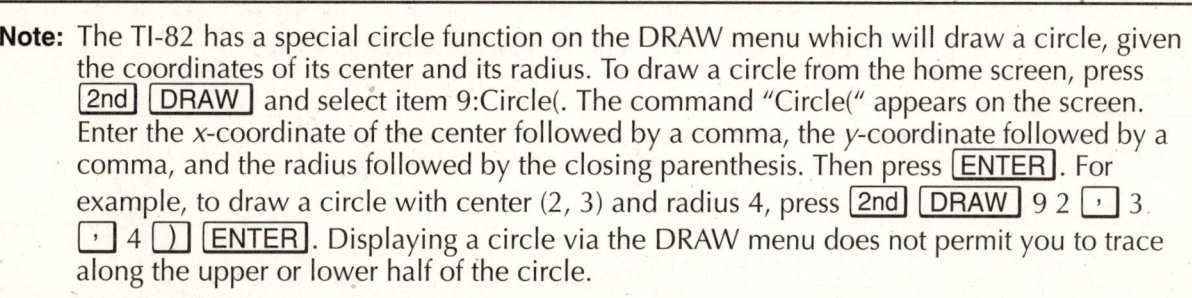

Note: The TI-82 has a special circle function on the DRAW menu which will draw a circle, given the coordinates of its center and its radius. To draw a circle from the home screen, press [2nd] [DRAW] and select item 9:Circle(. The command "Circle(" appears on the screen. Enter the *x*-coordinate of the center followed by a comma, the *y*-coordinate followed by a comma, and the radius followed by the closing parenthesis. Then press [ENTER]. For example, to draw a circle with center (2, 3) and radius 4, press [2nd] [DRAW] 9 2 [,] 3 [,] 4 [)] [ENTER]. Displaying a circle via the DRAW menu does not permit you to trace along the upper or lower half of the circle.

Trigonometric Functions and Their Inverses

● Casio fx-7700GE   ● TI-81   ● TI-82/83

A graphing calculator is a good tool for exploring the graphs of trigonometric functions and their inverses. Since a graphing calculator is capable of graphing trigonometric functions in degrees or radians, be sure that your calculator is in the correct mode for the function you wish to graph.

1   Graph $y = \cos x$ for $-360° \leq x \leq 360°$.

Casio: The Casio graphing calculators have several built-in functions that can be graphed with a minimum of keystrokes and without specifying the range values. The sine, cosine, and tangent functions are three of the built-in functions. To use a built-in function, press [Graph] and the name of the function only, do not enter x.

To put the Casio fx-7700GE in degree mode, press [SHIFT] [DRG] [F1] [EXE]. The viewing window is automatically set to $[-360, 360]$ by $[-1.6, 1.6]$ when the built-in cosine function is entered.

Press [Graph] [cos] [EXE].

TI: You must set the range values and then enter the equation for the function much as you would write it with pencil and paper. First, check to see that you are using degrees by pressing the [MODE] key. If not, use the arrow keys to select "Deg" (or "Degree") and press [ENTER]. You can then set the viewing window manually. If you wish, you can set the window automatically by pressing [ZOOM] 7. Press [RANGE] or [WINDOW] to see what settings your calculator uses for the viewing window.

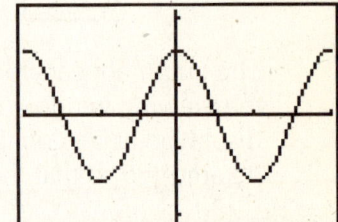

For the TI-81, press [Y=] [COS] [X|T] [GRAPH]. For the TI-82/83, press [Y=] [COS] [X,T,θ] [GRAPH].

2   Graph $y = 2 \sin \frac{1}{2} x$. Use the viewing window $[-540, 540]$ by $[-3, 3]$ with a scale factor of 90 for the x-axis and 1 for the y-axis.

Since the function is not one of Casio's built-in functions, you must set the viewing window manually.

Casio fx-7700GE: [Graph] 2 [sin] [(] [X,θ,T] [÷] 2 [)] [EXE]

TI-81: [Y=] 2 [SIN] [(] [X|T] [÷] 2 [)] [GRAPH]

TI-82/83: [Y=] 2 [SIN] [(] [X,T,θ] [÷] 2 [)] [GRAPH]

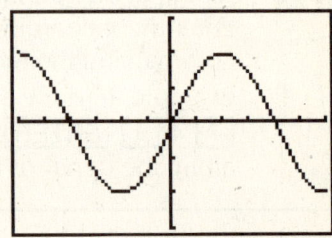

30

Graphing calculators can also graph the inverses of trigonometric functions.

3 **Graph $y = \text{Arccos } x$.**

Casio: Arcsin, Arccos, and Arctan are also built-in functions on Casio calculators, so you do not need to set the range.

Press [Graph] [SHIFT] [cos] [EXE].

TI: The range will need to be set on the TI calculator. A good window to use is $[-1, 1]$ by $[-20, 180]$ with a scale factor of 0.5 on the x-axis and 90 on the y-axis.

For the TI-81, press [Y=] [2nd] [COS] [XT] [GRAPH]. For the TI-82/83, press [Y=] [2nd] [COS] [X,T,θ] [GRAPH].

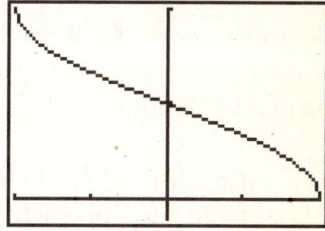

4 **Graph $y = \sin\left(\text{Sin}^{-1} x - \text{Cos}^{-1} \dfrac{x}{2}\right)$** in the viewing window $[-\pi, \pi]$ by $[-2, 2]$ with a scale factor of $\dfrac{\pi}{3}$ on the x-axis and $\dfrac{1}{2}$ on the y-axis.

Begin by putting your calculator in radian mode. On the Casio fx-7700GE, press [SHIFT] [DRG] [F2] [EXE]. On the TI calculators, access the mode menu and highlight "Rad" or "Radian" using the arrow keys and the [ENTER] key.

The Casio fx-7700GE and the TI-82/83 will allow you to enter operation symbols and constants like π directly into the range. If you are using a TI-81 calculator, you must manually enter a decimal approximation into the range.

Casio fx-7700GE: [Graph] [sin] [(] [SHIFT] [sin⁻¹] [X,θ,T] [−] [SHIFT] [cos⁻¹] [(] [X,θ,T] [÷] 2 [)] [)] [EXE]

TI-81: [Y=] [SIN] [(] [2nd] [SIN⁻¹] [XT] [−] [2nd] [COS⁻¹] [(] [XT] [÷] 2 [)] [)] [GRAPH]

TI-82/83: [Y=] [SIN] [(] [2nd] [SIN⁻¹] [X,T,θ] [−] [2nd] [COS⁻¹] [(] [X,T,θ] [÷] 2 [)] [)] [GRAPH]

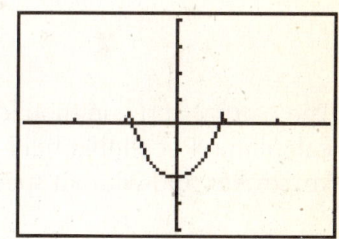

Exponential and Logarithmic Functions

● Casio fx-7700GE   ● TI-81   ● TI-82/83

A graphing calculator can be used to graph exponential and logarithmic functions just as it is used to graph other types of functions. Even functions that would be tedious and time consuming to draw by hand can be graphed quickly.

1 Graph $y = 9^{2+x}$ in the viewing window $[-7, 1]$ by $[-1, 9]$ with a scale factor of 1 on each axis.

Be sure that your calculator is in rectangular coordinate mode.

Casio fx-7700GE: [Graph] 9 [^] [(] 2 [+] [X,θ,T] [)] [EXE]

TI-81: [Y=] 9 [^] [(] 2 [+] [X|T] [)] [GRAPH]

TI-82/83: [Y=] 9 [^] [(] 2 [+] [X,T,θ] [)] [GRAPH]

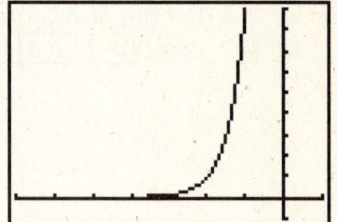

2 Graph $y = -\left(\frac{1}{2}\right)^{3-2x}$. Use the viewing window $[-5, 5]$ by $[-10, 2]$ with a scale factor of 2 on each axis.

Casio fx-7700GE: [Graph] [(−)] 0.5 [^] [(] 3 [−] 2 [X,θ,T] [)] [EXE]

TI-81: [Y=] [(−)] 0.5 [^] [(] 3 [−] 2 [X|T] [)] [GRAPH]

TI-82/83: [Y=] [(−)] 0.5 [^] [(] 3 [−] 2 [X,T,θ] [)] [GRAPH]

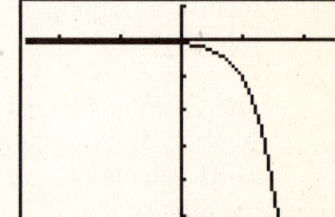

The natural and common logarithms are built-in functions on the Casio calculator. Recall that built-in functions can be graphed using a minimum of keystrokes and without specifying the range values.

3 Graph $y = \ln x$.

Casio: [Graph] [ln] [EXE]   *Remember that you do not enter x when using a built-in function on the Casio.*

TI: Set the viewing window on the TI to $[-1, 8]$ by $[-1, 3]$ with a scale factor of 1 on each axis.

TI-81: [Y=] [LN] [X|T] [GRAPH]

TI-82/83: [Y=] [LN] [X,T,θ] [GRAPH]

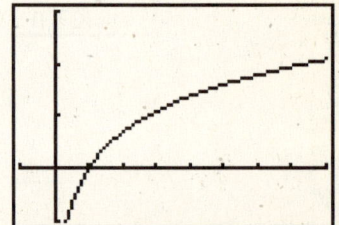

Graphing calculators can be used to graph logarithmic functions with base 10 or base *e*. If you wish to graph a logarithmic function with another base, you must use the change of base formula, $\log_a x = \dfrac{\log x}{\log a}$ or $\log_a x = \dfrac{\ln x}{\ln a}$.

4 Graph $y = \log_4 x$. Use the viewing window $[-1, 5]$ by $[-3, 3]$ with a scale factor of 1 on each axis.

Using the change of base formula, $\log_4 x = \dfrac{\log x}{\log 4}$.

Casio fx-7700GE: [Graph] [log] [X,θ,T] [÷] [log] 4 [EXE]

TI-81: [Y=] [LOG] [X|T] [÷] [LOG] 4 [GRAPH]

TI-82/83: [Y=] [LOG] [X,T,θ] [÷] [LOG] 4 [GRAPH]

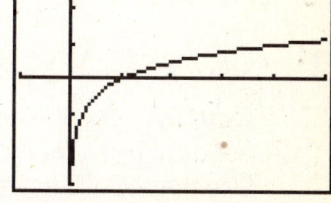

The graph of the equation has a vertical asymptote at $x = 0$. It may appear that the graph starts at $x = 0$, but actually the calculator cannot graph enough values to show the true behavior of the graph. As always, it is important to know how to interpret the graph that the calculator draws. The domain is $x > 0$, and the range is the set of real numbers.

5 Graph $y = -\log_6 (3 - x)$ in the viewing window $[-8, 4]$ by $[-5, 5]$ with a scale factor of 1 on each axis.

Casio fx-7700GE: [Graph] [(−)] [log] [(] 3 [−] [X,θ,T] [)] [÷] [log] 6 [EXE]

TI-81: [Y=] [−] [LOG] [(] 3 [−] [X|T] [)] [÷] [LOG] 6 [GRAPH]

TI-82/83: [Y=] [(−)] [LOG] [(] 3 [−] [X,T,θ] [)] [÷] [LOG] 6 [GRAPH]

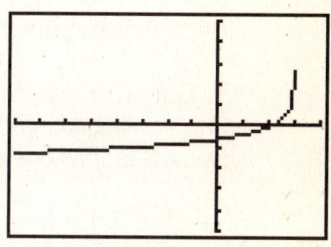

Application: Solving Equations in One Variable

● Casio fx-7700GE   ● TI-81   ● TI-82/83

You can use the graphs of two linear functions to solve an equation like $3x + 6 = 5x - 2$. For the first function, let $y =$ one side of the equation. For the second function, let $y =$ the other side of the equation. Then graph both equations on the same screen. The solution will be the x-coordinate of the point where the two functions intersect.

1 **Solve $3x + 6 = 5x - 2$ by graphing.**

Graph $y = 3x + 6$ and $y = 5x - 2$ on the same screen using the viewing window $[-3, 16]$ by $[-5, 25]$.
Use the TRACE function to find the approximate point of intersection. *The TRACE in the viewing window at the right shows the exact intersection point of the two lines. This may not occur with your calculator.*

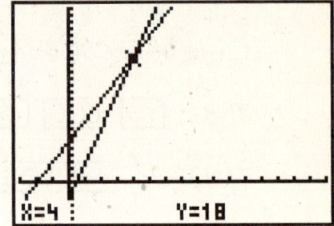

The x-coordinate is the solution to the equation.
Thus, the solution for $3x + 6 = 5x - 2$ is 4.

To review clearing graphs from the screen, refer to page 9.

2 **Solve $3x + 6 = 4x - (x - 10)$.**

Graph $y = 3x + 6$ and $y = 4x - (x - 10)$ on the same screen using the standard viewing window.

Notice that the lines do not appear to intersect.

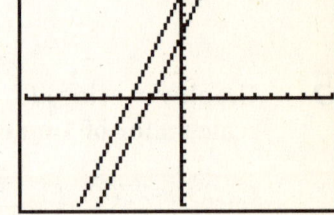

You may wish to zoom out on the graph to make sure that you are viewing a complete Remember that when the coefficients of x in linear equations are the same, the graphs of the equations are parallel lines.

Since the lines do not intersect, there is no solution.

3 **Solve $4(x + 2) = 6x + 2(4 - x)$.**

Graph $y = 4(x + 2)$ and $y = 6x + 2(4 - x)$ on the same screen using the standard viewing window. Notice that both graphs seem to coincide.

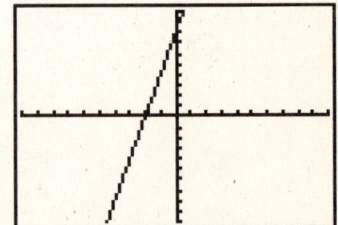

You may wish to zoom in on the graph to make sure that the graphs coincide. If you simplify each equation you will find they are equivalent. The graphs of equivalent equations are identical.

Since the graphs coincide, all real values of x satisfy both equations. The solution is all real numbers.

Note: The TI-82 has a special function on the CALC menu that will identify the point of intersection of two graphs. See the note at the bottom of page 19 for an explanation of the "intersect" feature.

Application: Solving Quadratic Equations

- Casio fx-7700GE   • TI-81   • TI-82/83

A quadratic equation is an equation in the form of $Ax^2 + Bx + C = 0$, where $A \neq 0$. The solutions for this type of equation can be estimated by graphing the related function, $y = Ax^2 + Bx + C$ and locating those points where $y = 0$. The x-coordinates of these points are called the **zeros** of the function. The zeros of a function are the *roots* to the associated equation.

1 Solve $2x^2 - x - 15 = 0$.

Graph $y = 2x^2 - x - 15$. Use a viewing window of $[-10, 10]$ by $[-16, 4]$.

Notice that the graph intersects the x-axis in two places. Therefore, there are two real solutions for the equation.

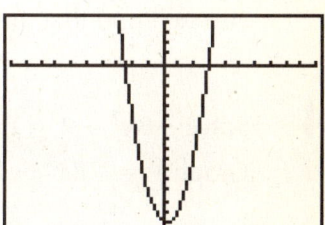

Use ZOOM and TRACE to find the points where the graph intersects the x-axis.

The graph intersects the x-axis at $(-2.5, 0)$. One solution for the equation is -2.5.

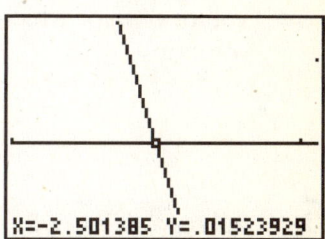

Continue to trace along the graph. The graph also intersects the x-axis at $(3, 0)$. Another solution for the equation is 3. *Always check your estimated solution.*

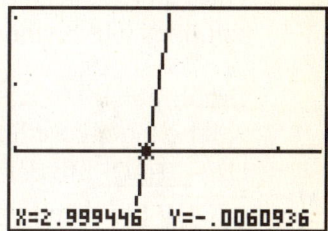

Note: The TRACE function can only give you the coordinates of the graph dot that appears to lie on the x-axis. Often you may not be able to find the exact x-coordinate for the point where the y-coordinate is zero.

2 Solve $x^2 - 10x + 25 = 0$.

Graph $y = x^2 - 10x + 25$.

Notice that the graph appears to intersect the x-axis at one point. Whenever there appears to be a single point of intersection, it is a good idea to zoom in on that point, because the graph could intersect the axis in two points very close together, or not intersect the axis at all.

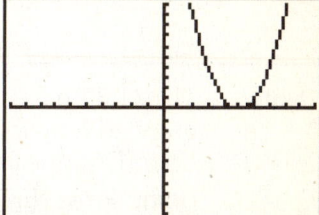

Zoom in on the point. Then use TRACE to determine the x-coordinate of the point where the graph intersects the x-axis.

The graph intersects the axis at $(5, 0)$.
The solution is 5.

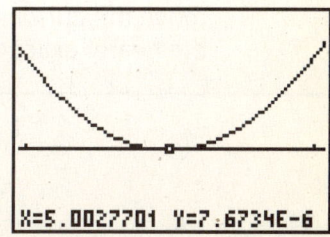

35

3 **Solve $10x^2 - 51x + 65 = 0$.**

Graph $y = 10x^2 - 51x + 65 = 0$.

The graph appears to intersect the x-axis at a single point between 2 and 3.

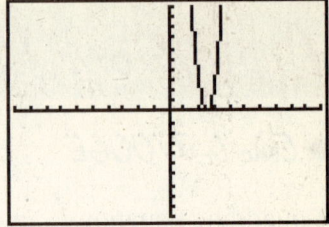

Zoom in on the point where the graph intersects the x-axis. After several zooms, you can see that the graph actually intersects the axis in two points. The x-coordinates of these points appear to be almost exactly 2.5 and 2.6. If you substitute the values 2.5 and 2.6 in the original equation, you will find that they are in fact exact solutions.

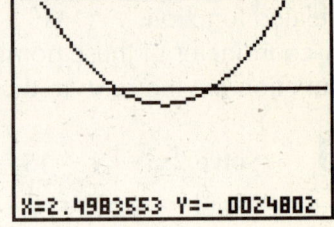

4 **Solve $-8x^2 - 1 = 0$.**

Graph $y = -8x^2 - 1$.

Notice that the graph does not intersect the x-axis. Therefore there are no values of x for which $y = 0$. Thus, the equation $-8x^2 - 1 = 0$ has no real solutions.

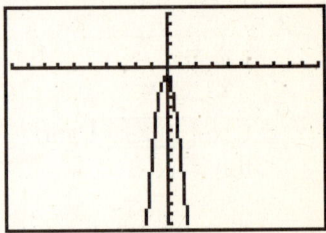

5 **Solve $x^2 + 3x + 5 = 2 - x$.**

This can be solved by treating each side of the equation as a function. The solutions will be those values of x that satisfy both functions.

Graph $y = x^2 + 3x + 5$ and $y = 2 - x$ on the same screen. The solutions will be the x-coordinates of the points where the tow graphs intersect. Use [TRACE] to determine the x-coordinate of each intersection. Use [ZOOM] to determine the most accurate estimates for x. The solutions are -3 and -1.

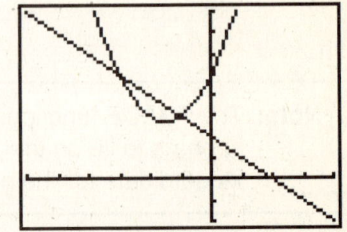

TI-82 note: The "intersect" function on the CALC menu can be used to find the coordinates of the points of intersection of two graphs. For more information, see page 19.

Note: The TI-82 has a special function on the CALC menu that will identify the x-intercept of the graphed function. When "2:root" is selected from the CALC menu, a prompt saying "Lower bound?" appears. Use ▶ or ◀ to move the cursor to a point just to the left of the apparent zero point. Press [ENTER]. The prompt "Upper bound?" appears. Move the cursor to a point just to the right of the estimated zero and press [ENTER]. A prompt saying "Guess?" appears, asking you to move the cursor as close as you can to the point you think the zero occurs. Press [ENTER] and the nearly exact coordinates of the actual x-intercept appear.

Application: Families of Graphs

- Casio fx-7700GE • TI-81 • TI-82/83

A family of graphs is a group of graphs that displays one or more similar characteristics. Many linear functions are related because they have the same slope or the same *y*-intercept as other functions in the family. All linear functions can be written in the form $y = mx + b$, where *m* represents the slope of the line and *b* is the *y*-intercept. You can graph several functions on the same screen and observe if any family traits exist.

1 Graph the following functions on the same screen. Then describe the family of graphs to which they belong.

$y = 0.5x + 1$
$y = x + 1$
$y = 3x + 1$
$y = 5x + 1$

Remember, to graph several functions on the same screen on the Casio calculator you must use a multistatement. Press [Graph], enter the equation, press [ALPHA] [:], then repeat the steps, connecting equations with the colon.

Use the standard viewing window.
When all functions are graphed on the same screen, you can observe that they are all lines and that they all pass through the point (0, 1). However, their slopes are different. If you compare each graph with its slope, you find the greater the slope, the greater the angle formed by the line and the *x*-axis. This family of graphs can be described as lines that have a *y*-intercept of 1.

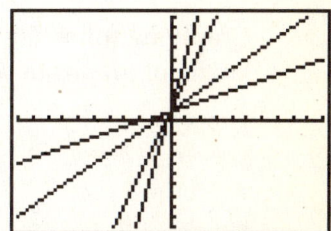

Note: On the TI calculators, you can suppress any of the graphs to observe each one in comparison to another. To do this, press [Y=]. Notice that the = sign in each equation is highlighted. Use the arrow keys to move the cursor over the = of the function you do not wish to graph. Press [ENTER]. Notice the = sign is no longer highlighted. That function will not be graphed when you press [GRAPH]. To graph the function again, use the arrow key to move to the = sign and press [ENTER] again. The = sign will once again be highlighted and the function will again be graphed.

2 Graph the following functions on the same screen. Then describe the family of graphs to which they belong.

$y = 3x$
$y = 3x + 1$
$y = 3x - 2$
$y = 3x + 5$

When all functions are graphed on the same screen, you can observe that they are lines that have different *y*-intercepts, but they appear to be parallel. Lines that are parallel have the same slope. This family of graphs can be described as lines that have a slope of 3.

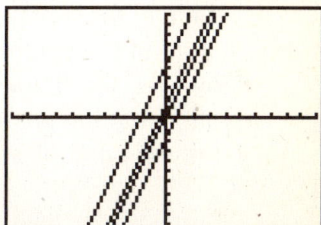

Note: On the TI-82/83, families of functions are easily graphed using the bracket keys, { and }, which are second functions of the parentheses keys. The brackets are used to group those numbers that change when all of the other parts of the equations are identical.

In Example 1, use the brackets to group the differing coefficients of x. Press [Y=] [2nd] [{] .5 [,] 1 [,] 3 [,] 5 [,] [}] [X,T,θ] [+] 1. Then press [GRAPH] and all of the functions will be graphed.

In Example 2, use the brackets to group the differing values of b. Press [Y=] 3 [X,T,θ] [+] [{] 0 [,] 1 [,] [(−)] 2 [,] 5 [}] [GRAPH].

Quadratic functions whose graphs are parabolas can be written in the form $y - k = a(x - h)^2$, where (h, k) represents the coordinates of the vertex of the parabola. As with lines, there are families of parabolas that share common characteristics. One family of parabolas may possess the identical shape, but have different vertices. Another family may have the same vertex, but the shapes of the parabolas differ.

3 **Graph the following functions on the same screen. Then describe the family of graphs to which they belong.**

$y = x^2$
$y = (x + 2)^2$
$y = (x - 4)^2 + 3$
$y = x^2 - 6$

When all the functions are graphed on the same screen, you can observe that the parabolas do not have the same vertex. However, all of the parabolas open upward and have the same shape. The shape can be described by the simplest function, $y = x^2$. This family of graphs can be described as parabolas with the shape of the graph of $y = x^2$, translated to different locations on the coordinate plane.

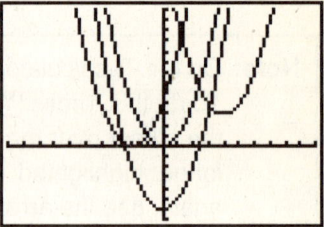

4 **Graph the following functions on the same screen. Then describe the family of graphs to which they belong.**

$y = -0.5x^2$
$y = -x^2$
$y = -4x^2$
$y = -8x^2$

When all the functions are graphed on the same screen, you can observe that all of the parabolas have the same vertex and open downward. However, the shapes of the parabolas differ with the coefficient of x^2. Notice that the greater the coefficient the narrower the opening. This is the family of parabolas that open downward and have a vertex at the origin.

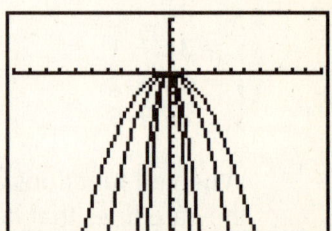

Application: Maxima, Minima, and Zeros of Functions

- Casio fx-7700GE
- TI-81
- TI-82/83

You can use the graphing calculator to estimate the zeros and the relative maximum and minimum points of a polynomial function. First you must graph the function. Then use TRACE and ZOOM to determine the coordinates of the point(s) you desire.

1 Approximate the maximum, minimum, and zeros of $y = -x^2 - 3x + 4$.

First graph the function.

The graph is a parabola opening downward that intersects the x-axis at two points. Therefore, the function has a maximum, no minimum, and two zeros.

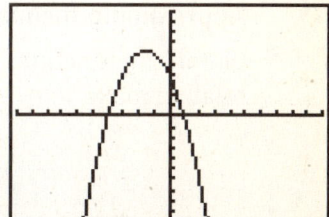

Use the TRACE function to locate the approximate coordinates of the maximum. Use the arrow keys to find the point where the y-coordinate displayed at the bottom of the screen appears to be greatest.

Remember that the coordinates that appear at the bottom of your calculator's screen may not match those shown at the right.

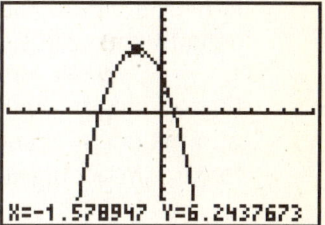

Once you have located the approximate maximum, use the ZOOM feature to enlarge your graph. Then use the TRACE function again to gain more precise coordinates. The maximum occurs at approximately $(-1.50, 6.25)$.

If you use the Box Zoom feature to create a rectangle similar in shape to that of the viewing window, the curve will maintain its parabolic shape while zooming in on the desired area.

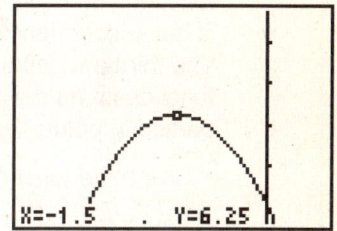

The coordinates of the zeros can be found in a similar way by using TRACE to find the point(s) where the graph crosses the x-axis and then using ZOOM to fine-tune your coordinate readings. The two zeros of this function are at approximately -4.00 and 1.00. If you substitute these values for x in the quadratic expression, you will find that they are, in fact, the exact zeros of the function.

> **TRACE Note:** Because graphing calculators differ, your readings may not match those given here. Remember that the TRACE function gives you the coordinates of the dots on the grid and not every value along the curve.

2 Approximate the maximum, minimum, and zeros of $y = 2x^3 + x^2 - 5x - 3$ to the nearest hundredth.

First graph the function.
The graph appears to have a relative maximum, a relative minimum, and three zeros. Use TRACE and ZOOM to refine your estimates of the coordinates of each point.

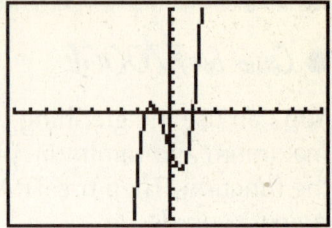

The relative maximum occurs at about $(-1.09, 1.05)$. The relative minimum occurs at about $(0.76, -5.34)$. The three zeros occur at about $-1.50, -0.62,$ and 1.62.

3 Approximate the maxima, minima, and zeros of $y = x^4 - 5x^2 + 6$.

Graph the function. The graph appears to have two relative minima, one relative maximum, and two zeros.

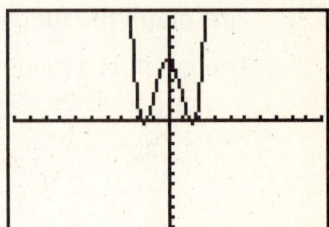

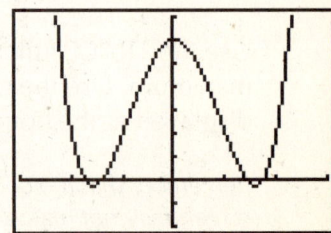

However, if you zoom in on the function, you will find that there are actually four zeros. These zeros are about $-1.73, -1.41, 1.41,$ and 1.73.

By zooming in on other parts of the curve, you will find the relative minima occur at about $(-1.58, -0.25)$ and $(1.58, -0.25)$. The relative maximum occurs at $(0, 6)$.

Note: The TI-82 and TI-83 have special functions that will find a zero, a minimum, or a maximum of the function you have graphed. These special functions can be accessed on the **CALC** menu, which is the second function of the TRACE key. The second item **2:root** finds the zero of a function. The third and fourth selections find the minimum and maximum, respectively. For each of these functions, you are asked to define the interval in which you wish the calculator to search for a particular point. The following directions apply to each function.

- Graph the function. Access the CALC menu.

- Select the point you wish to find (2:root, 3:minimum, or 4:maximum)

- Your graph will be displayed with a prompt at the bottom saying "Lower Bound?" Move the cursor to the point you wish to be the lower bound for the interval in which you wish to find a particular point. Press ENTER.

- A second prompt saying "Upper Bound?" will appear. Once again, move the cursor to the point which represents the upper bound of the interval in which you wish to find a particular point. Press ENTER.

- A third prompt saying "Guess?" appears. Move the cursor to the point at which you think the point occurs and press ENTER. The cursor will then move to the exact point and the x- and y- coordinates will appear at the bottom of the screen.

Application: Solving Trigonometric Equations

- Casio fx-7700GE   • TI-81   • TI-82/83

You can use a graphing calculator to solve a trigonometric equation in the same way you have used it to solve linear equations, quadratic equations, and systems of equations.

1 **Solve $\tan x = \sin x \cdot \cos x$ if $-360° \leq x \leq 360°$.**

Make sure your calculator is set for degree measure. Set the RANGE for x-values greater than the given interval, say $[-450°, 450°]$ with a scale factor of 90°. For the y-axis, use $[-3, 3]$ with a scale factor of 1.

Graph $y = \tan x$ and $y = \sin x \cdot \cos x$ on the same screen. Then use TRACE and ZOOM to locate the points of intersection in the interval $-360°$ to $360°$. The x-coordinates of those points are the solutions to the equation. The solutions are $-360°$, $-180°$, $0°$, $180°$, and $360°$.

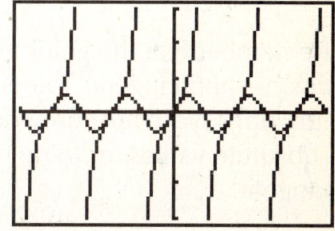

2 **Solve $2 \cos x - 4 = 0$ if $0° \leq x \leq 360°$.**

Set the RANGE for the viewing window $[-90°, 450°]$ by $[-8, 2]$. Since one side of the equation equals zero, you will use the method for finding the x-intercepts of a function.

Graph $y = 2 \cos x - 4$.

Notice the graph does not intersect the x-axis. There are no x-intercepts and, thus, no solutions for the equation.

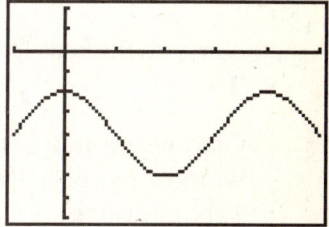

3 **Solve $\sin 3x + \cos 2x = 1$ if $0° \leq x \leq 360°$.**

Use the viewing window $[-90°, 450°]$ by $[-5, 5]$.

You can also solve the equation by first algebraically manipulating the equation to get 0 on the right-hand side: $\sin 3x + \cos 2x - 1 = 0$.

Graph $y = \sin 3x + \cos 2x - 1$. Then find the x-intercepts of the function by using TRACE and ZOOM. The solutions are $0°$, $40.6°$, $139.4°$, $180°$, and $360°$. *The decimal values are approximations.*

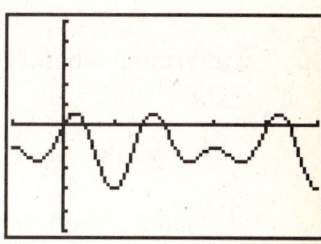

Application: Verifying Trigonometric Identities

- Casio fx-7700GE
- TI-81
- TI-82/83

You can use a graphing calculator to determine whether an equation may be a trigonometric identity by graphing each side of the equation as a separate function on the same screen and then comparing the two graphs. If the graphs appear to coincide, then the equation may be an identity. If the graphs do not match, then the equation is not an identity. Any equation must be verified algebraically to prove that it is an identity.

Remember that the graphing calculator only has function keys for the sine, cosine, and tangent. Therefore, if the identity you wish to verify contains other functions, you must use your knowledge of the basic trigonometric identities to substitute values for these trigonometric functions in terms of the sine, cosine, or tangent.

1 Determine whether $\tan x + \cot x = \sec x \cdot \csc x$ may be an identity.

First rewrite the equation in terms of the trigonometric functions available.

Since $\cot x = \frac{1}{\tan x}$, $\sec x = \frac{1}{\cos x}$, and $\csc x = \frac{1}{\sin x}$, the equation can be written as $\tan x + \frac{1}{\tan x} = \frac{1}{\cos x} \cdot \frac{1}{\sin x}$.

Graph each side of the equation on the same screen. Use the viewing window $[-360°, 360°]$ by $[-5, 5]$, with a scale of $90°$ for the x-axis and 1 for the y-axis.

The asymptotes may not appear on the screen of your calculator.

The graphs appear to coincide, so the equation may be an identity. You can verify algebraically that the equation is, in fact, an identity.

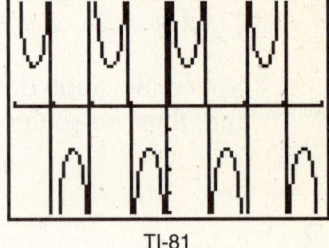
TI-81

2 Determine whether $\cot\left(\frac{x}{2}\right) = \frac{2 \cos x}{1 + 2 \sin x}$ may be an identity.

First, rewrite $\cot\left(\frac{x}{2}\right)$ as $\frac{1}{\tan\left(\frac{x}{2}\right)}$ en graph each side of the equation on the same screen. *Note that when entering $\tan\left(\frac{x}{2}\right)$, you must use parentheses around $x \div 2$ or the calculator will interpret the expression as $(\tan x) \div 2$.*

The graphs do not coincide. Therefore, the equation is not an identity.

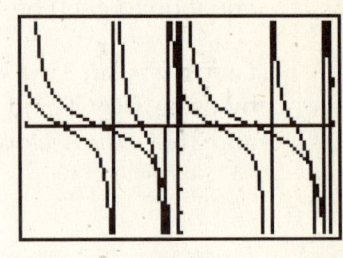
TI-81

Application: Solving Exponential and Logarithmic Equations

- Casio fx-7700GE
- TI-81
- TI-82/83

You can use a graphing calculator to solve equations involving logarithms and exponents just as you have used it to solve other types of equations. There are two methods: (1) graph each side of the equation and find the intersection points or (2) rewrite the equation so that it equals zero, graph the related function, and find the x-intercepts of the function. For exponential and logarithmic equations, the second method is often easier because it is easier to see where the graph crosses the x-axis than it is to see the point(s) of intersection. Often a point of intersection is near an asymptote and the gradual decrease or increase can make that point of intersection difficult to find.

1 Solve $\left(\frac{1}{4}\right)^{3x} = 6^{x-2}$.

Use the viewing window $[-2, 4]$ by $[-3, 3]$.

First transform the equation so that one side equals zero. That is $\left(\frac{1}{4}\right)^{3x} - 6^{x-2} = 0$. Graph $y = \left(\frac{1}{4}\right)^{3x} - 6^{x-2}$.

Then use TRACE and ZOOM to locate the x-intercept.

The solution is approximately 0.6.

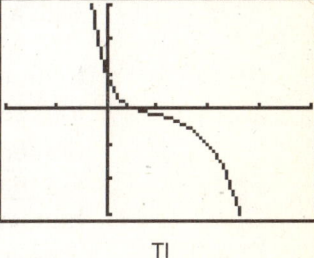
TI

You could solve the equation using the first method to verify your solution.

2 Solve $\log(x + 3) = \log(7 - 4x)$.

Use the viewing window $[-5, 5]$ by $[-3, 3]$.

Transform the equation to $\log(x + 3) - \log(7 - 4x) = 0$.

Graph the equation and use TRACE and ZOOM to locate the x-intercept.

The solution appears to be very close to 0.8. You can use substitution to confirm that 0.8 is the exact solution.

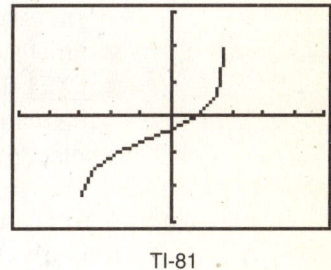
TI-81

Note: To solve exponential or logarithmic inequalities, use the methods described on pages 21 and 22.

Entering Matrices

● *Casio fx-7700GE*   ● *TI-81*   ● *TI-82/83*

Graphing calculators make many of the tedious paper-and-pencil operations with matrices quick and simple. Each calculator has different matrix capabilities, but they all work through matrix menus. Suppose you wanted to enter the matrix $\begin{bmatrix} 1 & 3 & -6 \\ 2 & -2 & 4 \end{bmatrix}$.

Casio fx-7700GE: The Casio fx-7700GE contains memories for five different matrices and a special matrix answer memory. You can enter values into matrices A through E. The answer matrix is used to store the result of a matrix operation. The maximum dimensions for each matrix is 9 rows by 9 columns.

Before entering a matrix, you must be in matrix mode. Press [MENU] 5 and then press [F4]. The matrix list will be displayed.

To select matrix A, press [F1]. The last elements of matrix A appear along with a different menu at the bottom of the screen.

If this matrix A has the same dimensions as the one you wish to enter, you can proceed by entering the elements of the desired matrix. Press 1 [EXE] 3 [EXE] – 6 [EXE] 2 [EXE] –2 [EXE] 4 [EXE]. As you press each number, it appears at the bottom of the screen. When you press [EXE], the number appears in the matrix, and the highlight moves on to the next element to be entered.

```
A    1    2    3
1  [ 1    3   -6 ]
2  [ 2   -2    4 ]
```

If matrix A does not have the same dimensions as the one you wish to enter, you can change the dimensions by pressing [F2] which designates the dimensions of the matrix. Enter the appropriate number of rows and then press [EXE]. Then enter the number of columns and press [EXIT]. You will return to the matrix list showing a 2 × 3 matrix. Follow the directions given above to select matrix A and enter the correct numbers.

You can enter another matrix in the same way, but select matrix B instead of matrix A on the first matrix menu.

TI-81: The TI-81 contains memories for three matrices, A, B, and C. You can enter values into all three matrices and use them in operations. Each matrix has a maximum dimension of 6 × 6. There is no matrix mode on the TI calculators.

To enter a matrix, press [MATRX]. A menu of matrix operations appears. Use the arrow key to go to the EDIT menu. A list of three matrices and their dimensions appears. Select whichever matrix you wish by using the up and down arrows to highlight your selection and press [ENTER].

```
MATRIX   EDIT
1: [A]    6 × 6
2: [B]    3 × 2
3: [C]    3 × 3
```

44

If the matrix you chose has the same dimensions as the matrix you wish to enter, press ENTER twice. Element 1, 1 (row 1, column 1) is highlighted. Enter the number you want and press ENTER. Continue the process until all values are entered.

```
[A] 2 × 3
1,1 = 1
1,2 = 3
1,3 = −6
2,1 = 2
2,2 = −2
2,3 = 4
```

If the matrix you chose does not have the same dimensions as the matrix you wish to enter, press the number for the number of rows and ENTER. Then press the number of columns and ENTER. Proceed as shown above to enter each element.

When you finish entering the values of your matrix, press 2nd QUIT. The home screen appears. To view the matrix, press 2nd [A], which is the second function of the 1 key. Then press ENTER. The matrix will appear on the screen. *Notice that the second functions of the 2 and 3 keys, access matrices B and C, respectively.*

```
[A]
[1   3  −6]
[2  −2   4]
```

You can enter the other two matrices in the same way, by selecting the appropriate matrix on the EDIT menu.

TI-82:

The TI-82 has memories for five matrices, *A, B, C, D,* and *E.* You can enter values into all five matrices. The maximum dimensions for each matrix is 99 × 99.

Entering a matrix on a TI-82 calculator is similar to the process described for the TI-81. To enter a matrix, press MATRX and use the arrows to highlight EDIT. The list of five matrices appears. Use the up and down arrows to select whichever matrix you wish to define and press ENTER. You change the dimensions of the matrix in the same way as the TI-81.

Once the matrix dimensions are defined, a matrix of those dimensions appears on the screen. In a newly-defined matrix, all the values are zeros. In a previously-defined matrix, the values are those entered when the matrix was defined. The first element (row 1, column 1) is highlighted. Enter the first value and press ENTER. Then use the arrow keys to move to the new value you wish to enter. When you have completed the entries, you can exit the screen by pressing 2nd QUIT.

```
MATRIX [A] 2 × 3
[1    3   −6]
[2   −2    4]


1,1 = 1
```

Note: If you enter a large matrix, not all of the columns and/or rows may appear on the screen. To view other portions of the matrix, you can use the arrow keys to scroll to the portion of the matrix you wish to view.

Determinants, Inverses, and Operations

● Casio fx-7700GE   ● TI-81   ● TI-82/83

The graphing calculator has simplified the tasks of finding determinants and inverses of matrices to the pressing of only a few keys.

1 Find the determinant of matrix A if $A = \begin{bmatrix} 1 & 3 \\ 2 & -2 \end{bmatrix}$.

Enter the matrix into your calculator.

Casio fx-7700GE: Press [EXIT] [EXIT] [F2] [F1] [ALPHA] A [EXE].
The determinant appears.
Press [F1] [ALPHA] A [F5] to return to the original matrix screen.

TI-81: Press [MATRX]. Then select 5:det. Then name the matrix you want by pressing [2nd] [[A]] and [ENTER] to calculate the determinant.

TI-82/83: From the home screen, press [MATRX] and use the arrow keys to highlight the MATH menu. Use the arrow keys to highlight item 1:det and press [ENTER]. To select the matrix, press [MATRX] and highlight the NAMES menu. Use the arrow key to highlight the matrix you want and press [ENTER]. Press [ENTER] again to perform the calculation.

The determinant of matrix A is -8.

2 Find the inverse of matrix A if $A = \begin{bmatrix} 1 & 3 \\ 2 & -2 \end{bmatrix}$.

Casio fx-7700GE: Press [F1] [ALPHA] A [SHIFT] [x^{-1}] [EXE].
The inverse appears.
Press [F1] [ALPHA] A [F5] to return to the original matrix screen.

TI-81: Press [2nd] [[A]] [x^{-1}] [ENTER].

TI-82/83: Press [MATRX] and select the matrix you want as described above in Example 1. Press [x^{-1}] and [ENTER] to perform the calculation.

The inverse of matrix A is $\begin{bmatrix} 0.25 & 0.375 \\ 0.25 & -0.125 \end{bmatrix}$.

```
[A]⁻¹
[.25    .375]
[.25   -.125]
```
TI-81

Other operations with matrices that can be done with a graphing calculator include scalar multiplication, multiplying two matrices, squaring a matrix, adding and subtracting two matrices, and finding the transpose of a matrix.

Casio fx-7700GE: Once you have entered matrices A and B, you can add the two matrices, subtract the two matrices, and multiply the two matrices.

$A + B$ Press [F1] [ALPHA] A [+] [F1] [ALPHA] B [EXE]. The sum appears.

$A - B$ Press [F1] [ALPHA] A [−] [F1] [ALPHA] B [EXE]. The difference appears.

$A \times B$ Press [F1] [ALPHA] A [X] [F1] [ALPHA] B [EXE]. The product appears.

Every time you do a calculation, the result is automatically stored in the matrix answer. If you wish to use the results for another computation, press [EXIT] [◄] [►]. You can then assign the matrix to C, D, or E for further computations.

To perform scalar multiplication, first input the multiplier, then select the matrix you want to multiply and press [EXE]. The result appears automatically.

TI: To perform operations with matrices, you enter them in an expression in the same way you would enter a variable and execute the calculation by pressing [ENTER]. The only difference in the operation of the two calculators is how the matrices are called up into the expression.

To multiply matrices A and B on the TI-81, select matrix A by pressing [2nd] [[A]]. Then press [X] and select matrix B by pressing [2nd] [[B]]. The expression [A] × [B] appears in the window. Press [ENTER] to calculate the result.

To add matrices A and B on the TI-82, you must use the NAME menu on the MATRX menu to name each matrix as it is needed. The other operations are the same as with the TI-81.

Note: On the TI-82/83, matrix expressions involving several operations are easy. Enter the expressions in much the same form as you would write them. Evaluating a matrix expression such as $3A + 4B$ on the TI-81 or Casio fx-7700GE requires storing of intermediate results and additional keystrokes. See the manual for your calculator for tips on evaluating such expressions.

Statistical Computations

- Casio fx-7700GE   • TI-81   • TI-82/83

In addition to graphing, graphing calculators are capable of doing intricate computations, including finding statistical values for a set of data. The first step on the Casio fx-7700GE is to choose the appropriate statistical mode for statistical computations. This mode is called standard deviation mode. Press [MENU] 3. You may choose to store the data for computations or to use the data once and discard it. We will use the data storage mode. Enter data storage mode by pressing [SHIFT] [SET UP] [▼] [▼] [F1]. The keystrokes for non-storage mode are [SHIFT] [SET UP] [▼] [▼] [F2].

You must clear all of the statistical memories on your calculator before performing any computations. If you forget to clear the memories, your calculations may include old data values causing your results to be incorrect.

Casio fx-7700GE: [SHIFT] [CLR] [F2]   Clears the data in the memory.

TI-81: [2nd] [STAT] [◄] 2 [ENTER]   Clears the data in the memory.

TI-82/83: [STAT] 4 [2nd] [L1] [ENTER] [STAT] 4 [2nd] [L2] [ENTER]   Clears data lists L1 and L2.

1 The prices for several bicycle helmets are given below. Find the mean, the standard deviation, and the sum of the data. Then find the sum of the squares of the data values and the standard deviation of a population for which the data is a sample.

51	40	58	60	30	45	66	40	87	65
41	60	40	35	47	49	54	50	52	47

Enter the data into the calculator.

Casio fx-7700GE: 51 [F1] 40 [F1] 58 [F1] and so on 47 [F1]

> To correct a mistake in the data on a Casio fx-7700GE, press [F2] to access the data edit menu. Then locate the incorrect data value with the arrow keys, type in the correct data, and press [EXE].

TI-81: Before you enter new data, clear any data that may have been stored in the calculator. To do this, press [2nd] [STAT] [◄] 2 [ENTER]. Data is always entered as a data pair. So, when you wish to analyze a set of single data points, the y-value of the data pair represents the frequency of the occurrence of the x-value. For example, the data pairs (9, 1) and (11, 3) represent one occurrence of the data value 9 and three occurrences of the data value 11. When the data memory is cleared all y-values are set to 1, so pressing [ENTER] when the cursor is on the y-value will accept this frequency.

[2nd] [STAT] [◄] [ENTER]   *Accesses the data edit option.*

51 [ENTER][ENTER][ENTER] 40 [ENTER][ENTER] 58
[ENTER][ENTER] *and so on* 47 [ENTER] [ENTER]

TI-82/83: Data is entered individually into a list. Before you enter new data, clear data that may have been previously stored in data list L1. Press [STAT] 4 [2nd] [L1] [ENTER]. Use the following procedure to enter the new data.

[STAT][ENTER]   *Accesses the data edit option.*
51 [ENTER] 40 [ENTER] 58 [ENTER] *and so on* 47 [ENTER]

If you make a mistake entering data into your TI calculator, use the arrow keys to move to the incorrect data and enter the correct value. If you wish to delete an incorrect data point on a TI-81, move the cursor to the " = " for the *x*- or *y*-value of the point and press [DEL]. Pressing [INS] when the cursor is on the " = " allows you to insert a new data pair before that point. On a TI-82, you can delete data by moving the cursor to the data to be deleted and pressing [DEL]. To insert data at a desired point, press [2nd] [INS] and enter the data.

Now that the data is entered, we can find the statistical values.

Casio fx-7700GE: [F4] [F1] [EXE]   *Chooses the mean from the standard deviation function menu and calculates.*

[F2] [EXE]   *Chooses the standard deviation from the standard deviation function menu that is already displayed and calculates.*

[EXIT] [F5] [F2] [EXE]   *Exits to the previous menu, enters the data sum function menu, then chooses and calculates the sum.*

[F1] [EXE]   *Chooses the sum of the squares from the data sum menu that is already displayed.*

[EXIT] [F4] [F3] [EXE]   *Exits to the previous menu, enters the standard deviation function menu, then chooses and calculates the standard deviation of the population.*

TI-81: [2nd] [STAT] [ENTER][ENTER]   *Chooses 1-VAR from the statistics calc menu.*

TI-82/83: [STAT] [▶] 1 [ENTER]

Notice that the TI calculators display many statistics at one time. $\bar{x}$ denotes the mean, Σx is the sum, Σx^2 is the sum of the squares, Sx is the standard deviation of a population for which the data is a sample, σx is the standard deviation of the data given, and n is the number of data values. The TI-82 and TI-83 provide additional statistical results.

To the nearest hundredth, the mean of the data is 50.85, the standard deviation is 12.59, the sum is 1017, the sum of the squares is 54,885, and the standard deviation of a population for which the data is a sample is 12.92.

```
1-Var
x̄ = 50.85
Σx = 1017
Σx² = 54885
Sx = 12.9178579
σx = 12.59077043
n = 20
```
TI-81

2 **Find the median of the test scores listed below on a TI calculator.**

82	91	74	78	94	68	74	88	64	42
72	82	79	99	98	75	61	78	86	69

Only the Casio fx-7700GE and the TI-82/83 graphing calculators will compute the median of a set of data for you. However, the TI-81 calculator will sort data from least to greatest according to the *x*- or *y*-values so that the median can be found easily.

Note: On the TI-81, the y-values must all be 1 for this technique to be accurate.

Clear the data memory and enter the data into your calculator.

Casio fx-7700GE: [F2] [F3] [F1]   *Clear the data memory.*

82 [F1] 91 [F1] 74 [F1] *and so on* 69 [F1]

[F4]   *Chooses the standard deviation function menu.*

[F4] [F2] [EXE]   *Chooses the median from the representative menu and calculates.*

TI-81: [2nd] [STAT] [◄] 2 [ENTER]   *Clear the data memory.*

[2nd] [STAT] [◄] 82 [ENTER] [ENTER]
[ENTER] *and so on* 69 [ENTER]   *Choose the data edit option and enter the data.*

TI-82/83: [STAT] 4 [2nd] [L1] [ENTER]   *Clear data list L1.*
[STAT] [ENTER] 82 [ENTER]   *Choose the data edit option and enter the data.*
and so on 69 [ENTER]

TI-81: Now sort the data using the xSort option under the statistics data menu.

[2nd] [STAT] [◄] 3 [ENTER]

We have 20 pieces of data, so the median is the average of the 10th and 11th values. We can use the [{x}] key, located above the 0 key, to recall the *x*-value of a data point when we enter the number of the data point in the set. This will allow us to find the mean of the 10th and 11th values.

[(] [2nd] [{x}] 10 [)] [+] [2nd] [{x}] 11 [)] [)] [÷] 2 [ENTER]

TI-82/83: Find the single variable statistics.

[STAT] [►] [ENTER] [ENTER]

Use the down arrow key to scroll down to read the median value which is listed as Med = .

The median test score is 78.

Histograms

- Casio fx-7700GE   • TI-81   • TI-82/83

A graphing calculator is capable of drawing statistical graphs as well as graphs of functions. The Casio calculator must be placed in statistical graph draw mode before statistical graphs can be drawn. To do this, press [MENU] 3 then [SHIFT] [SET UP] [▼] [▼] [▼] [F1].

Before starting each graph, it is important to clear the statistical memory. Since only one set of data can be stored at a time, not clearing the memory could cause you to enter your new data into an old data set and produce incorrect graphs. To clear the data memory, press [F2] [F3] [F1] on the Casio fx-7700GE; on a TI-81, press [2nd] [STAT] [◄] 2 [ENTER]; and on a TI-82/83, press [STAT] 4 [2nd] [L1] [ENTER].

1 Use a graphing calculator to create a histogram of the data listed below.

Class Limits	Frequency	Class Limits	Frequency
95–110	3	185–200	24
110–125	7	200–215	15
125–140	15	215–230	11
140–155	34	230–245	7
155–170	42	245–260	4
170–185	38		

You must set the range for the graph. Use the range values [95, 260] by [0, 50] with scale factors of 15 on the x-axis and = on the y-axis. A TI calculator will use the Xscl value as the width of the bars that will be drawn to automatically determine the number of bars. The Casio calculator requires that you specify the number of bars you wish to display. Since there are 11 classes, we will set the calculator to display 11 bars. Press [SHIFT] [Defm] 11 [EXE].

Now enter the data into the memory and draw the graph. The class mark, that is the midpoint of the class, is entered as the first number in each data pair. For example, for the class limits 95–110, enter 102.5. The class frequency is entered as the second number in each data pair. If you are using a Casio calculator, the numbers in the data pairs must be separated by a semicolon.

Casio fx-7700GE: 102.5 [F3] 3 [F1] 117.5 [F3] 7 [F1] 132.5 [F3] 15 [F1] 147.5 [F3] 34 [F1] *and so on* 252.5 [F3] 4 [F1] [Graph] [EXE]   *Draws the graph.*

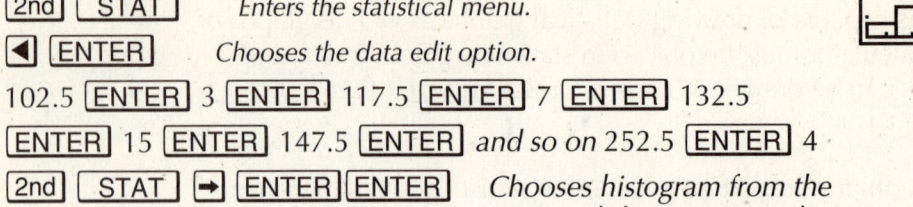

TI-81: [2nd] [STAT]   *Enters the statistical menu.*
[◄] [ENTER]   *Chooses the data edit option.*
102.5 [ENTER] 3 [ENTER] 117.5 [ENTER] 7 [ENTER] 132.5 [ENTER] 15 [ENTER] 147.5 [ENTER] *and so on* 252.5 [ENTER] 4
[2nd] [STAT] [→] [ENTER] [ENTER]   *Chooses histogram from the statistical draw menu and executes.*

TI-82: The TI-82 requires that the class marks be entered as data list L1 and the frequencies be entered as data list L2.

[STAT] [ENTER]   *Enters the data edit menu.*
102.5 [ENTER] 117.5 [ENTER] *and so on* 252.5 [ENTER]   *Enter the class marks in L1.*
[►] 3 [ENTER] 7 [ENTER] *and so on* 4 [ENTER]   *Then enter the frequencies in L2.*
[2nd] [STAT PLOT] [ENTER]   *Chooses the statplot menu.*

Use the arrow and [ENTER] keys to highlight "On". Then choose the histogram with L1 as the Xlist and L2 as the Frequency. Press [GRAPH] to plot the histogram.

2 **Use a graphing calculator to create a histogram of the data listed below using a class interval of 10. Then make a second histogram using class intervals of 15.**

84	120	78	89	107	116	73	88	106	117
144	92	100	124	84	100	115	76	93	112
89	109	110	128	101	109	135	100	112	81
99	119	88	117	110	81	103	127	97	120
93	115	92	116	68	97	66	102	84	115

For the histogram with class intervals of 10, set the range to [60, 150] by [0, 20] with scale factors of 10 on the *x*-axis and 2 on the *y*-axis. Set the number of bars to 9 on the Casio calculator by pressing [SHIFT] [Defm] 9 [EXE].

Clear the statistical memory and then enter the data and graph. Since each data piece is a single value, each *y*-value will be 1. There is no need to enter the *y*-value into the Casio calculator when the *y*-value is 1. You can simply enter the *x*-value and press [F1].

Casio fx-7700GE: 84 [F1] 120 [F1] 78 [F1] 89 [F1] *and so on*
 115 [F1] [Graph] [EXE]

TI-81: The calculator also enters 1 as the second value of the data pair automatically, so you can press [ENTER] to accept this value instead of entering 1 for each *y*-value.

[2nd] [STAT] [◀] 1   *Chooses the data edit option.*
84 [ENTER] [ENTER] 120 [ENTER] [ENTER] 78 [ENTER] [ENTER]
89 [ENTER] [ENTER] *and so on* 115
[2nd] [STAT] [▶] 1 [ENTER]   *Chooses histogram from the statistical draw menu and executes.*

TI-82/83: [STAT] [ENTER]   *Chooses the data edit option.*
84 [ENTER] 120 [ENTER] 78 [ENTER] 89 [ENTER] *and so on* 115 [ENTER]
[2nd] [STAT PLOT] [ENTER]   *Chooses the statplot menu.*

Use the arrow and [ENTER] keys to highlight "On", the histogram, "L1" as the Xlist, and "1" as the frequency. Press [GRAPH] to complete the histogram.

Now make the second histogram using class intervals of 15.

Casio fx-7700GE: When generating a new histogram of the same data on the Casio fx-7700GE, you must change the number of bars to be drawn, and if necessary change the Xscl value in the range. If the range has not been changed, you must clear the graphics screen, clear the calculated statistical values, and recalculate the statistical values before you can regraph with new class intervals. Be sure to complete each step or the new graph that is drawn will be incorrect.

[SHIFT] [Defm] 6 [EXE]   *Changes the number of bars.*
[Range] [EXE] [EXE] 15   *Changes the Xscl value to 15.*
[EXE] [Range] [Range]   *Exits the range menu.*
[SHIFT] [CLR] [F2] [EXE]   *Clears the calculated statistical values.*
[F6]   *Recalculates the statistical values with the new intervals.*
[Graph] [EXE]   *Completes the graph.*

TI: On the TI calculators, you can simply change the Xscl value in the range to 15. Then press [2nd] [STAT] [▶] 1 [ENTER] on a TI-81 or press [GRAPH] on a TI-82 to graph the same data with new class intervals.

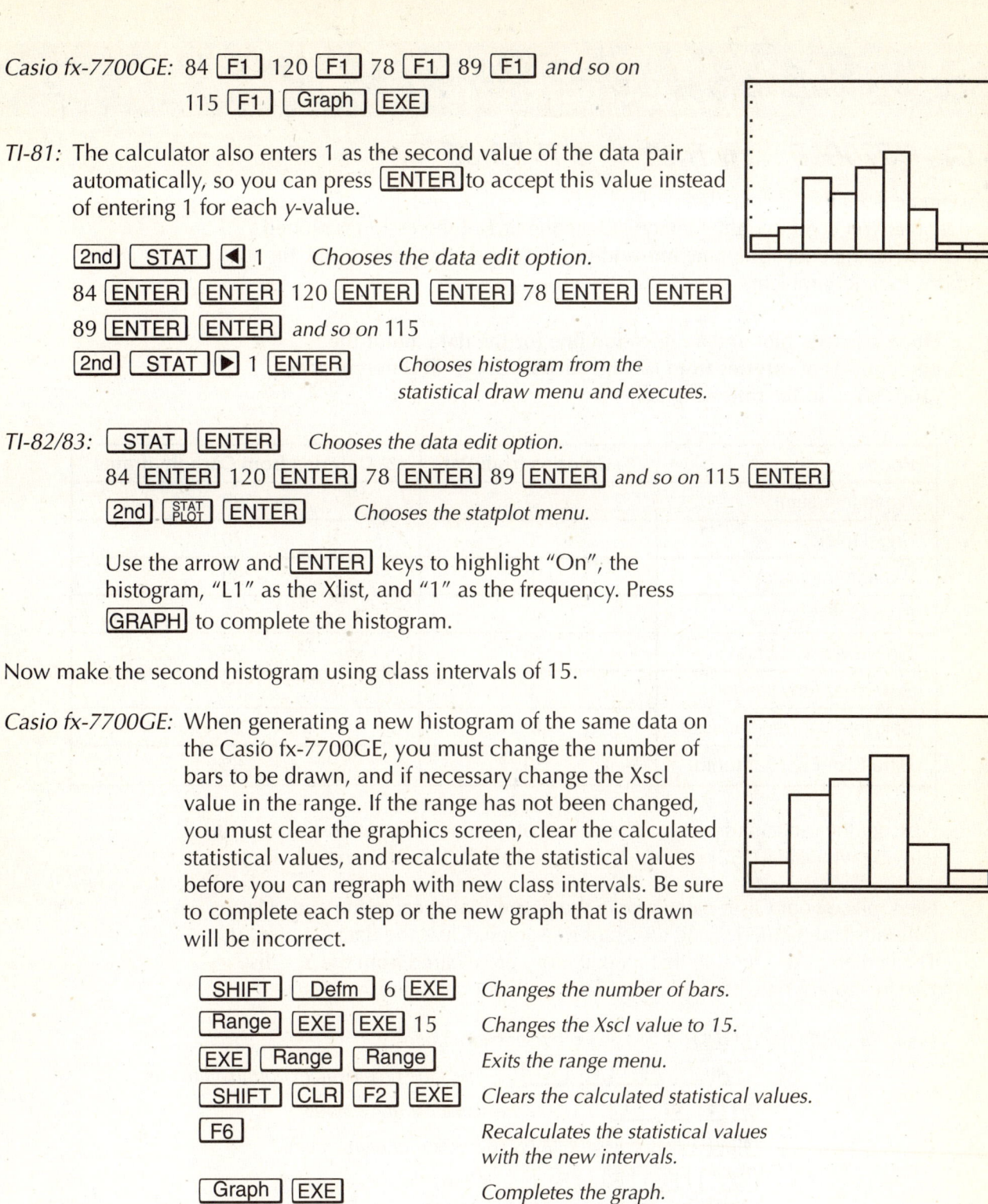

Scatter Plots and Lines of Regression

- Casio fx-7700GE   • TI-81   • TI-82/83

Graphing calculators are capable of drawing scatter plots and lines of regression for data that you enter into the memory. Once the line of regression is plotted, you can write the equation of the line and use the trace function to approximate solutions to other problems.

1 Draw a scatter plot and a regression line for the data about the percentages of calories from fat and carbohydrates in different snack foods given in the following table.

Food	% Calories from Fat	% Calories from Carbohydrates
Apple (medium)	9	89
Bagel (plain)	6	76
Banana (medium)	2	93
Bran Muffin (large)	40	53
Fig Newtons (4 bars)	18	75
PowerBar (any flavor)	8	76
Snickers bar (regular size)	42	51
Ultra Slim-Fast bar (one)	30	63

First, set the range parameters. The values of the data suggest that we use the viewing window [0, 50] by [50, 100] with scale factors of 5 on both axes.

Next, place your Casio calculator in the proper statistical mode and clear the statistical memories and the graphics screen. Clear the data list of your TI calculator. Also be sure that all equations are cleared from the Y = list. Use the appropriate keystrokes below to set your calculator.

Casio fx-7700GE: [MENU] 4   Sets the regression mode.
　　　　　　　　　　[SHIFT] [SET UP] [F1]   Sets the rectangular coordinate mode.
　　　　　　　　　　[▼] [▼] [▼] [F1]   Sets the statistical draw mode.
　　　　　　　　　　[▼] [F1]   Sets the linear regression drawing mode.
　　　　　　　　　　[EXIT] [F2] [F3] [F1]   Clears the data memory.
　　　　　　　　　　[SHIFT] [CLR] [F2] [EXE]   Clears the statistical memory.
　　　　　　　　　　[SHIFT] [Cls] [EXE]   Clears the graphics screen.

TI-81:   [2nd] [STAT] [◄] 2 [ENTER]   Clears the statistical memory.

TI-82/83:   [STAT] 4 [2nd] [L1] [2nd] [L2] [ENTER]

Now you can enter the data. The Casio calculator will plot the points as you enter them.

Casio fx-7700GE: 9 [F3] 89 [F1] 6 [F3] 76 [F1] *and so on* 30 [F3] 63 [F1]

TI-81: [2nd] [STAT] [◀] [ENTER]   *Chooses the data edit option.*
9 [ENTER] 89 [ENTER] 6 [ENTER] 76 [ENTER] *and so on* 30 [ENTER] 63 [ENTER]

TI-82/83: [STAT] [ENTER]   *Chooses the data edit option.*
9 [ENTER] 6 [ENTER] 2 [ENTER] *and so on* 30 [ENTER]   *Enters first list into L1.*
[▶] 89 [ENTER] 76 [ENTER] 93 [ENTER] *and so on* 63 [ENTER]   *Enters second list into L2.*

Now draw the regression line.

Casio: [Graph] [SHIFT] [F4] 1 [EXE]

TI-81: [2nd] [STAT] 2 [ENTER]   *Calculates the coefficients of the regression line.*
[Y=] [VARS] [▶] [▶] 4 [ENTER] [GRAPH]   *Writes the equation of the regression line in Y= list and graphs the line.*
[2nd] [STAT] [▶] 2 [ENTER]   *Draws the scatter plot.*

TI-82/83: [2nd] [STAT PLOT] [ENTER]   *Chooses the statplot menu.*

Use the arrow and [ENTER] keys to highlight "On", the scatterplot, "L1" as the Xlist, and "L2" as the Ylist and "." as the mark. Press [GRAPH] to see the scatterplot.

[STAT] [▶] 9 [ENTER]   *Calculates coefficients of the regression line.*
[Y=] [VARS] 5 [▶] [▶] 7 [GRAPH]   *Writes regression line equations in the Y = list and graphs.*

The TI-81 calculates coefficients a and b for a regression equation of the form $y = a + bx$. The TI-82/83 uses the form $y = ax + b$. The Casio uses $y = A + Bx$. The value of r tells you how well the line fits the data. The r-value of -0.939 for the example problem shows that the line has a good fit and that the x- and y-values are inversely proportional. To display values of A, B, and r on a Casio fx-7700GE, press [G↔T] [F6] [F1] [EXE] [F2] [EXE] [F2].

A, B, and r correspond to the [F1], [F2], and [F3] keys, respectively.

2 Use the trace feature on the regression line in Example 1 to predict the percentage of calories from carbohydrates for a food which has 27% of its calories from fat.

Activate the trace feature. If you have performed any other operations on your Casio calculator since you graphed the line, you will have to regraph before the trace feature will be available.

Casio: [SHIFT] [F1]   *TI:* [TRACE]

Use the arrow keys to move the cursor to a point on the regression line that has an x-coordinate of approximately 27. From the regression equation, a food with 27% of its calories from fat has approximately 65% of its calories from carbohydrates.

Curve Fitting

- Casio fx-7700GE • TI-81 • TI-82/83

Some sets of data do not display a linear pattern when plotted on a scatter plot. A set of data that is fit best by a curve is called *curvilinear* data. Since most real-world data are positive, most scatter plots are graphed in the first quadrant. If the points of these data sets are connected, the graph might resemble an exponential graph of the form $y = Ae^{Bx}$ or a polynomial graph of the form $y = Ax^B$.

Since the graphs of exponential functions and polynomial functions can have similar characteristics in the first quadrant, it is often difficult to distinguish between a quadratic, a cubic, or an exponential function with simple observation. Since it is too difficult to determine what type of function a scatter plot may resemble by looking at the data points, it is best to try both equations and see which one fits better.

1 Use the population data shown in the table below to determine the exponential equation that best fits the data and describe the goodness of fit.

Years since 1780	Population (in millions)	Years since 1780	Population (in millions)	Years since 1780	Population (in millions)
10	3.9	80	31.4	150	123.2
20	5.3	90	38.6	160	132.2
30	7.2	100	50.2	170	151.3
40	9.6	110	63.0	180	179.3
50	12.8	120	76.2	190	203.3
60	17.0	130	92.2	200	226.5
70	23.2	140	106.1	210	248.7

To simplify the values along the x-axis, define x in terms of the number of years since 1780.

First set the range parameters. A viewing window of [0, 225] by [0, 275] with scale factors of 25 for both axes is appropriate.

Next, set your calculator in the proper statistical mode and clear the statistical memories and the graphics screen. Also, clear any equations from the Y= list on the TI.

Casio fx-7700GE: [MENU] 4   *Sets the regression mode.*
　　　　　　　　　　[SHIFT] [SET UP] [F1]   *Sets the rectangular coordinates graph mode.*
　　　　　　　　　　[▼] [▼] [▼] [F1]   *Sets the statistical draw mode.*
　　　　　　　　　　[▼] [F3]   *Sets the exponential regression curve drawing mode.*
　　　　　　　　　　[EXIT] [SHIFT] [CLR] [F1] [EXE]   *Clears the entire memory.*
　　　　　　　　　　[SHIFT] [Cls] [EXE]   *Clears the graphics screen.*

TI-81: [2nd] [STAT] [◀] 2 [ENTER]   *Clears the statistical memory.*

TI-82/83: [STAT] 4 [2nd] [L1] [ENTER] [STAT] 4 [2nd] [L2] [ENTER]

Then input the data.

Casio fx-7700GE: [EXIT] 10 [F3] 3.9 [F1] *and so on*
　　　　　　　　　　210 [F3] 248.7 [F1]

TI-81: [2nd] [STAT] [◀] [ENTER] 10 [ENTER] 20 [ENTER] *and so on*
　　　　210 [ENTER] 248.7 [ENTER]

TI-82/83: [STAT] [ENTER] 10 [ENTER] 20 [ENTER] *and so on* 210
　　　　　　[ENTER] [▶] 3.9 [ENTER] 5.3 [ENTER] *and so on* 248.7 [ENTER]

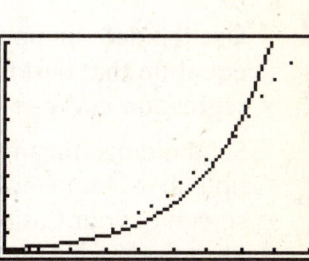

Regression curve (TI)

Now draw the scatter plot and curve of regression.

Casio: [Graph] [SHIFT] [F4] 1 [EXE]

TI-81: [2nd] [STAT] [▶] 2 [ENTER] [2nd] [STAT] 4 [ENTER]
　　　　[Y=] [VARS] [▶] [▶] 4 [GRAPH] [2nd] [STAT] [▶] 2 [ENTER]

TI-82/83: [2nd] [STAT PLOT] [ENTER]   *Chooses the statplot menu.*

Regression curve (Casio)

Highlight "On", the scatterplot, "L1" as the Xlist, and "L2" as the Ylist, and "." as the mark. Press [GRAPH] to see the scatterplot.

[STAT] [▶] [ALPHA] [A] [ENTER] [Y=] [VARS] 5 [▶] [▶] 7 [GRAPH]

57

On the TI calculators, the equation of the regression curve is
$y = 4.721 \times 1.02^x$, where $a = A$, and $b = x^B$. Pressing [LN] [VARS] [▶]
[▶] 2 [ENTER] on the TI-81 and [LN] [VARS] 5 [▶] [▶] 2 [ENTER] on the
TI-82/83 will give the value of B. The equation then can be written as
$y = 4.721e^{0.0208x}$.

On the Casio fx-7700GE, press [G↔T] [F6] [F1] [EXE] [F2] [EXE] to
display the values of A and B. The equation for the regression curve is then
$y = 4.721e^{0.0208x}$.

Pressing [G↔T] [F6] [F3] [EXE] on the Casio fx-7700GE, [VARS] [▶] [▶]
3 [ENTER] on the TI-81, or [VARS] 5 [▶] [▶] 6 [ENTER] on the TI-82 to
display the Pearson product-moment correlation value for the regression
equation. For this example, the value is 0.9836. From this, we can
conclude that the regression curve is an extremely good fit for the data.

A procedure similar to the one used for an exponential regression curve is used to
determine a polynomial equation to fit a set of data. The equation will be of the
form $y = Ax^B$.

2   **Use the data on populations given in Example 1 to find a polynomial
equation that best fits the data. Determine whether the exponential
regression curve or the power regression curve fits the data best.**

Set the range parameters to [0, 225] by [0, 275] with scale factors of 25 on
both axes. Remember to clear the statistical memories and the graphics
screen of your Casio calculator. Clear the exponential regression equation
from the Y= list, but do not clear the memories of your TI calculator since
the data does not need to be reentered.

Next enter the power regression mode on the Casio calculator.

Casio fx-7700GE: [SHIFT] SET UP [▼] [▼] [▼] [F4]

Now draw the scatter plot on the regression curve or line.

Casio: [EXIT] [F6] [Graph] [SHIFT] [Line] 1 [EXE]

TI-81: [2nd] [STAT] [▶] 2 [ENTER] [2nd] [STAT] 5 [ENTER] [Y=] [VARS] [▶] [▶] 4 [GRAPH] [2nd] [STAT] [▶] 2 [ENTER]

TI-82/83: [STAT] [▶] [ALPHA] [B] [ENTER]
[Y=] [CLEAR] *Clears the exponential equation from the Y = list.*
[VARS] 5 [▶] [▶] 7 [GRAPH]

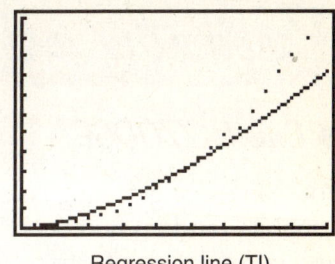

Regression line (TI)

As long as the statplot menu has not been changed, the scatterplot will still be displayed.

Using a TI calculator, the equation for the regression curve is $y = 0.0444 \times x^{1.5579}$, where $A = a$ and $b = B$.

On the Casio fx-7700GE, find the values of A and B by pressing [G↔T] [F6] [F1] [EXE] and [F2] [EXE]. The equation of the regression curve is then $y = 0.0444x^{1.5579}$.

To determine whether the exponential or the power regression model fits the data better, compare the Pearson product-moment correlation values. We determined that $r = 0.9836$ for the exponential model. Press [F3] [EXE] on the Casio fx-7700GE or [2nd] [STAT] 5 [ENTER] on the TI calculator to find r. The value of r for the power regression model is 0.9710. Therefore, the exponential model fits the data better.

Note: Remember that since it is often difficult to determine whether a scatter plot is best fitted by a power equation or an exponential equation, it is advisable to apply both processes to the data and compare the Pearson product-moment correlation values to determine which one fits the data best. If you are using a TI-81 calculator, this is easily done by pressing [2nd] [STAT] 4 [ENTER] for the exponential model and [2nd] [STAT] 5 [ENTER] for the power model after the data is entered. If you are using a TI-82, find the values by pressing [STAT] [▶] [ALPHA] [A] for the exponential model and [STAT] [▶] [ALPHA] [B] for the power model. On a TI-83, you can find the values by pressing [STAT] [▶] 0 for the exponential model and [STAT] [▶] [ALPHA] [A] for the power model. You do not need to draw a scatter plot or graph the equations to find the *r*-values.

Probability and Combinatorics

● Casio fx-7700GE   ● TI-81   ● TI-82/83

You can use a graphing calculator to find permutations and combinations and to generate random numbers. These capabilities are useful in finding probabilities and in modeling situations to study probability.

1 Find 12!.

    Casio fx-7700GE: 12 [SHIFT] [MATH]   Enter the number and access MATH menu.
                                     [F2]   Access the probability function menu.
                                     [F1] [EXE]   Choose x! and execute.

    TI-81:   12 [MATH]   Enter the number and access the MATH menu.
               5 [ENTER]   Choose option 5, !, and calculate.

    TI-82/83:   12 [MATH]   Enter the number and access the MATH menu.
                  [◄] 4 [ENTER]   Choose ! from the PRB menu and calculate.

The value of 12! is 479,001,600.

2 Find the value of P(9, 5).

    Casio fx-7700GE: Notice that if you just finished finding the factorial in Example 1, the probability function menu is already displayed. So you can just press [F2] for the permutation.

                             9 [F2] 5 [EXE]   Enter n, choose permutation, enter r, and execute.

    TI: 9 [MATH]   Enter n and access MATH menu.
          [◄] 2   Access the PBR menu and choose permutation.
          5 [ENTER]   Enter r and calculate.

The value of P(9, 5) is 15,120.

3 What is the probability that two cards drawn at random from a standard deck of 52 cards are both hearts?

$$P(\text{two hearts}) = \frac{C(13, 2)}{C(52, 2)}$$

Casio fx-7700GE: (13 [F3] 2) ÷ (52 [F3] 2) [EXE]

TI: (13 [MATH] ◄ 3 2) ÷ (52 [MATH] ◄ 3 2) [ENTER]

The probability that the cards are hearts is 0.06 to the nearest hundredth.

> **Hint:** You can display a calculated probability as a fraction on a Casio fx-7700GE by pressing [a b/c] instead of [÷] in the expression line. You can display the answer as a fraction on the TI-82/83 after calculating the decimal answer by pressing [MATH] 1 [ENTER]. As a fraction, the probability is $\frac{1}{17}$. There are limitations on the size denominators the calculators can handle when you wish to express the result of a computation in fraction form. If the denominator is too large, the calculator will leave the answer in decimal form.

The random number generators in graphing calculators will produce pseudo-random numbers. The numbers are close enough to being random for most purposes. The Casio calculator will find three-digit numbers between 0 and 0.999. The TI calculators will find numbers up to ten-digits long that are greater than 0 and less than 1. You will probably use the random number generator mainly in programming. *For a program using the random number generator, see page 69.*

4 Use the random number generator to find three random numbers.

Casio fx-7700GE: If you have just finished the combinations in Example 3, the probability function menu is still displayed. Press [F4] to activate the random number generator.

[F4] [EXE] [EXE] [EXE]

TI: [MATH] ◄ 1 [ENTER] [ENTER] [ENTER]

61

GRAPHING CALCULATORS IN THE SCIENCE CLASSROOM

Using Programs

type the omitted line. When you have finished entering the program, press [2nd] [QUIT] to exit the program edit menu.

When you are ready to execute a program, access the program menu, highlight EXEC, enter the number of the program you wish to run, then press [ENTER]. For example to execute program 1, press [PRGM] 1 [ENTER] If you need to stop a program while it is executing, press and hold the [ON] key until the program stops. This will bring up the error screen. To go to the program edit screen, press 1. To go to the home screen, press 2.

For instructions on erasing a program, refer to the manual for the calculator you are using. Likewise, for detailed instructions on entering, editing, and running programs, see the appropriate pages in the manual's chapter on programming.

Like larger computers, a graphing calculator can be used to write and run programs. The programs that follow will run on the TI-82 and the TI-83 calculators, but could be adapted easily for use on another type of graphing calculator or for a computer that runs BASIC or PASCAL.

To enter a program on the TI-82/83, press [PRGM], highlight NEW, and press [ENTER]. Type the program name and press [ENTER]. Enter the program pressing [ENTER] at the end of each statement.

The first line lists the program number and title. Type in the title and press [ENTER]. Then enter the program pressing [ENTER] at the end of each line. Refer to the calculator manual or the Appendix to find unfamiliar keystrokes. Note that any command that is written with lower case letters is generated using a calculator key or menu option. Most programming commands such as Goto, If, Disp, and Input are accessed by pressing the [PRGM] key while in the program edit mode. The alpha-lock, accessed by pressing [2nd] [A-LOCK], is similar to the shift-lock on a typewriter. Using alpha-lock makes all subsequent characters alpha characters. Cancel alpha-lock by pressing [ALPHA]. If you make a mistake while entering a program, correct it just as you would correct any other expression that you enter into the calculator. To insert a line you have accidentally omitted, use the arrow keys to place the cursor at the end of the line before the omitted line. Then press [2nd] [INS] [ENTER] and

62

Plotting Points in a Relation

The following program will plot the points in a relation.

Name = PLOTPTS

:Fn Off	*Deactivates all current functions.*
:ClrDraw	*Clears the graphics screen.*
:Lbl 1	*Sets the marker at position 1.*
:Disp "X="	*Displays the message "X=".*
:Input X	*Accepts an X value.*
:Disp "Y="	
:Input Y	
:PT-On(X,Y)	*Plots the point (X, Y).*
:Pause	*Waits until the user presses the ENTER key.*
:Disp "PRESS 0 TO QUIT OR 1 TO PLOT MORE POINTS"	
:Input A	
:If A = 0	*Tests to see if the entered value is 0.*
:End	*If A = 0, the program ends.*
:Goto 1	

Solving a System of Linear Equations

The program below will solve a system of two linear equations written in the form $Ax + By = C$ and $Dx + Ey = F$.

Name = SLVSYSTM

:Disp "FIRST X-COEFFICIENT="	*Displays the quoted message.*
:Input A	*Accepts a value for A.*
:Disp "FIRST Y-COEFFICIENT="	
:Input B	
:Disp :FIRST CONSTANT="	
:Input C	
:Disp "SECOND X-COEFFICIENT="	
:Input D	
:Disp "SECOND Y-COEFFICIENT="	
:Input E	
:Disp "SECOND CONSTANT="	
:Input F	
:If AE − BD = 0	*If the determinant of the coefficients is zero,*
:Goto 1	*the program will go to "Lbl 1."*
:(CE − BF)/(AE − BD) → X	*Value is calculated and stored for X.*
:Disp X	
:(AF − CD)/(AE − BD) → Y	*Value is calculated and stored for Y.*
:Disp Y	
:Goto 2	*Program will go to "Lbl 2."*
:Lbl 1	
:Disp "INCONSISTENT OR DEPENDENT"	
:Lbl 2	

Using the Quadratic Formula

The following program will find the solutions to a quadratic equation using the quadratic formula. The solutions will be given in decimal form.

Name = QUADRATC
:Disp "ENTER A, B, C FOR"
:Disp "AX² + BX + C = 0"
:Input A
:Input B
:Input C
:(B² − 4AC) → D   *Finds discriminant of D.*
:If D > 0   *Tests to see if D > 0.*
:Then
:Disp "TWO ROOTS"
:Disp (−B+ √ D)/(2A)   *Finds and displays one solution.*
:Disp (−B− √ D)/(2A)   *Finds and displays the second solution.*
:Else
:Goto 1
:Lbl 1
:If D=0   *Tests to see if D=0.*
:Disp "DOUBLE ROOT"
:Disp −B/(2A)
:Else
:Goto 2
:Lbl 2
:Disp "IMAGINARY"
:Disp "M+NI AND M+NI"
:Disp "PRESS ENTER"
:Disp "TO SEE M and N"
:Pause
:Disp "M="
:Disp −B/(2A)   *Finds and displays the real part of the solution.*
:Disp "N="
:Disp √ (abs D)/(2A)   *Finds and displays the imaginary part of the solution.*
:Stop

Using the Law of Cosines

This program finds the measure of a side of a triangle using the law of cosines. In the program, A is the measure of the missing side, B and C are the measures of the second and third sides, and θ is the measure of the angle opposite side A.

Name = LAWCOS

:Deg	*Places the calculator in degree mode.*
:Disp "INPUT B"	
:Input B	
:Disp "INPUT C"	
:Input C	
:Disp "INPUT θ"	
:Input θ	
:$\sqrt{(B^2 + C^2 - 2BC \cos \theta)} \to A$	*Calculates the value of A.*
:Disp "A="	
:Disp A	
:End	

Using Heron's Formula

The program below finds the area of a triangle using Heron's formula. You must enter the measures of all three sides of the triangle.

Name = HERONS

:Disp "ENTER SIDE"	
:Disp "LENGTHS A, B, C"	
:Input A	
:Input B	
:Input C	
:(A + B + C)/2 → S	*Calculates the semiperimeter and stores it in S.*
:S(S − A)(S − B)(S − C) → M	
:If M ≤ 0	*Uses triangle inequality to be sure that a triangle exists*
:Then	*for the given lengths.*
:Disp "NO TRIANGLE"	
:Else	
:Disp "AREA ="	
:Disp $\sqrt{M}$	
:End	

Inner and Cross Products of Vectors

Program 6 can be used to find the inner product of two vectors in a plane or in space. The program will indicate that the vectors are perpendicular if the inner product is 0. Program 7 below calculates the cross product of two vectors in space.

Name = INNRPROD
:Disp "INPUT 1 FOR PLANE"
:Disp "INPUT 2 FOR SPACE"
:Input I
:0 → C
:0 → F
:Disp "INPUT COORDINATES"
:Disp "VECTOR 1"
:Input A
:Input B
:If I = 1
:Then
:Goto 1
:Else
:Input C
:Lbl 1
:Disp "INPUT COORDINATES"
:Disp "VECTOR 2"
:Input D
:Input E
:If I = 1
:Then
:Goto 2
:Else
:Input F
:Lbl 2
:AD + BE + CF → P   *Calculates the inner product.*
:Disp "INNER PRODUCT"
:Disp P
:If P = 0
:Disp "PERPENDICULAR"
:Stop

Name = XPRODUCT
:ClrHome
:Disp "1ST VECTOR, A1="
:Input A
:Disp "A2="
:Input B
:Disp "A3="
:Input C
:Disp "2ND VECTOR, B1="
:Input D
:Disp "B2="
:Input E
:Disp "B3="
:Input F
:BF − EC → I   *Calculates i coefficient, stores in I.*
:DC − AF → J
:AE − BD → K
:Disp "CROSS PRODUCT"
:Disp "COEFF. OF I="
:Disp I
:Disp "COEFF. OF J="
:Disp J
:Disp "COEFF. OF K="
:Disp K
:Stop

Sum of a Series

The following program will find the sum of the first *n* terms of an arithmetic or geometric series. You will enter the type of series, the first term, the difference for an arithmetic series or the ratio for a geometric series, and the number of terms.

Name = SUMSER

:Disp "INPUT 1 FOR ARITHMETIC OR 2 FOR GEOMETRIC"
:Input T
:Disp "FIRST TERM"
:Input A
:Disp "DIFFERENCE OR RATIO"
:Input D
:Disp "NUMBER OF TERMS"
:Input N
:If T = 1
:Then
:N/2*(2A + (N−1)D) → S   *Finds the sum of the arithmetic series.*
:Goto 1
:Else
:(A − AD^N)/(1 − D) → S   *Finds the sum of the geometric series.*
:Lbl 1
:Disp "SUM ="
:Disp S

Sums in Summation Notation

This program will evaluate a sum in summation notation. Store the formula for the *n*th term in Y_1. You will input the values for the lower and upper bounds.

Name = SIGMASUM

:ClrHome
:Disp "NTH TERM MUST"
:Disp "BE IN Y1"
:Disp "LOWER BOUND ="
:Input L
:Disp "UPPER BOUND ="
:Input U
:0 → S   *Sets the initial sum value to 0.*
:L → X   *Stores the lower bound in X.*
:Lbl 1
:S + Y_1 → S   *Adds the value of Y_1 to the previous sum value.*
:X + 1 → X   *Increments X by 1.*
:If X = U + 1   *Checks to see if upper bound has been reached.*
:Goto 2
:Goto 1
:Lbl 2
:Disp "SUM = "
:Disp S

Graphical Iteration

This program will perform graphical iteration of a logistic function, which is of the form $f(x) = ax(1 - x)$. Press ENTER for values and to advance the graph. Before you run the program, set the range to [0, 1] by [0, 1] with scale factors of 0.1 on both axes. **Note:** To put "Fix 3" on the second line of the program, press MODE, highlight 3 after FLOAT on the second line, then press ENTER.

Name = GRITERAT

:ClrDraw
:Fix 3
:Disp "A ="
:Input A
:Disp "I ="
:Input I
:DrawF AX(1 − X)
:DrawF X
:0 → M
:0 → C
:If C = 0
:Then
:Goto 2
:Else
:Lbl 1
:AI − AII → I
:M + 1 → M
:If M < C
:Goto 1
:Goto 3
:Lbl 2
:Line(I, 0, I, I)
:Lbl 3
:AI − AII → J
:Line (I, I, I, J)
:Line (I, J, J, J)
:Pause
:Disp J
:Pause
:J → I
:M + 1 → M
:If M < C + 15
:Then
:Goto 3

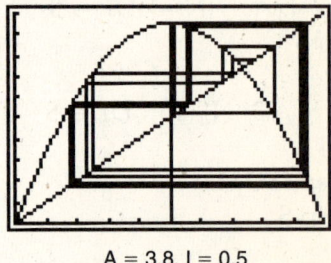

A = 3.8, I = 0.5

Mandelbrot Set

Use the following program to draw a rough picture of the Mandelbrot set. Before you run the program, set the range to [−2.6, 1.0] by [−1.2, 1.2] with scale factors of 0.5 on both axes. **Note:** This program will take about 20 minutes to run.

Name = MANDELBR

:Fnoff
:ClrDraw
:DispGraph
:0.0379 → C
:0.0381 → D
:0 → J
:Lbl J
:−1.2 + JD → B
:0 → I
:Lbl I
:−2.6 + IC → A
:A → X
:B → Y
:1 → K
:Lbl 1
:X^2 → U
:Y^2 → V
:2XY + B → Y
:U − V + A → X
:K + 1 → K
:If U + V > 100
:Goto 2
:If K < 15
:Goto 1
:PT-On(A, B)
:PT-On(A, −B)
:Lbl 2
:IS > (I, 95)
:Goto I
:IS > (J, 31)
:Goto J
:End

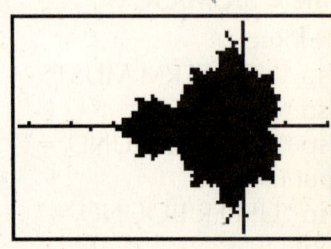

IS > (is a program control instruction that can be accessed from the program editor.

Generating Random Numbers

The following program will generate random numbers between two values. You input the seed number, which determines the way in which the numbers are generated. Note that the program will not eliminate duplicate numbers, and the factory set seed number is 0. Entering the least and greatest integers of 1 and 6 can simulate rolling one die, or entering 1 and 2 can simulate tossing a coin.

Name = RANDNUM
:ClrHome
:Disp "LEAST INTEGER"
:Input S
:Disp "GREATEST INTEGER"
:Input L
:Disp "SEED NUMBER"
:Input N
:Disp "NUMBER OF VALUES TO GENERATE"
:Input A
:0 → B
:N → Rand   *Sets a staring point in the random number table.*
:Lbl 1
:B + 1 → B
:Int ((L − S + 1)Rand + S) → R   *Calculates value of random number and stores.*
:Disp R
:Pause   *Waits until user presses ENTER.*
:If A ≠ B   *Tests if enough numbers have been generated.*
:Goto 1

Evaluating a Function

The program below will compute the value of a function that is stored in Y_1 for a given value of X. To end the program, press [2nd] [QUIT].

Name = TABLE
:Lbl 1
:Disp "X="
:Input X
:Disp "Y="
:Disp Y_1 *Displays the value of Y_1 using the input value of X.*
:Goto 1

Area Between Two Curves

The following program will approximate the area between the graphs of two functions by dividing the region into rectangles. Store the two functions as Y_1 and Y_2 in the Y= list. The program requires you to input the lower and upper bounds and the number of rectangles to use for the calculation.

Name = AREACRVE

:ClrHome
:"abs $(Y_1 - Y_2)$" $\to Y_3$ *Finds the average height of a rectangle.*
:Disp "LOWER BOUND ="
:Input L
:Disp "UPPER BOUND ="
:Input U
:Disp "NUMBER OF RECTANGLES"
:Input R
:$(U-L)/R \to W$ *Finds the width of each rectangle.*
:$L \to X$ *Sets the first value of X equal to L.*
:$Y_3 \to C$ *Stores the height of rectangle at X = L as C.*
:$0 \to N$ *Sets rectangle counter to 0.*
:$0 \to A$ *Sets area to 0.*
:Lbl 1
:$N + 1 \to N$ *Increase the rectangle counter by 1.*
:$X + W \to X$ *Adds width to X to determine next X.*
:$A + WY_3 \to A$ *Adds area to current total area.*
:If N = R   *Tests whether all rectangles were added.*
:Goto 2
:Goto 1
:Lbl 2
:$U \to X$ *Sets X to value of upper bound.*
:$Y_3 \to D$ *Stores height at X + U in D.*
:$A + WC - WD \to B$ *Calculates area using left endpoints.*
:$(A + B)/2 \to E$ *Averages two areas.*
:Disp "AREA ="
:Disp E
:End

Mickey Mouse

The following program will draw a picture of Mickey Mouse. The program was written by Ryan Kovacik, a sophomore at Strongsville High School in Strongsville, Ohio. It was printed in the April 1991 issue of *Mathematics Teacher*. Before running the program, set the viewing window to [6.5, 33.5] by [8, 32] with scale factors of 40 on both axes and clear any equation from the Y= list.

Name = MICKEY

:ClrDraw
:Shade $(28 - \sqrt{(16 - (X - 28)^2)}, 28 + \sqrt{(16 - (X - 28)^2)})$
:Shade $(28 - \sqrt{(16 - (X - 12)^2)}, 28 + \sqrt{(16 - (X - 12)^2)})$
:Shade $(14 - (1/2)\sqrt{(4 - (X - 20)^2)}, 14 + 0.5\sqrt{(4 - (X - 20)^2)})$
:Shade $(18 - (3/2)\sqrt{(1 - (X - 18)^2)}, 18 + 1.5\sqrt{(1 - (X - 18)^2)})$
:Shade $(18 - (3/2)\sqrt{(1 - (X - 22)^2)}, 18 + 1.5\sqrt{(1 - (X - 22)^2)})$
:Shade $(14 + (2/3)\sqrt{(9 - (X - 27)^2)}, 20 + (7/8)\sqrt{(64 - (X - 20)^2)})$
:Shade $(14 + (2/3)\sqrt{(9 - (X - 13)^2)}, 20 + (7/8)\sqrt{(64 - (X - 20)^2)})$
:Shade $(20 + 2\sqrt{(4 - (X - 22)^2)}, 20 + (7/8)\sqrt{(64 - (X - 20)^2)})$
:Shade $(20 + 2\sqrt{(4 - (X - 18)^2)}, 20 + (7/8)\sqrt{(64 - (X - 20)^2)})$
:DrawF $18.5 + (5/2)\sqrt{(1 - (X - 22)^2)}$
:DrawF $18.5 - (5/2)\sqrt{(1 - (X - 22)^2)}$
:DrawF $18.5 + (5/2)\sqrt{(1 - (X - 18)^2)}$
:DrawF $18.5 - (5/2)\sqrt{(1 - (X - 18)^2)}$
:DrawF $15 + (1/3)\sqrt{(9 - (X - 20)^2)}$
:DrawF $22 + \sqrt{(1 - (X - 22)^2)}$
:DrawF $22 + \sqrt{(1 - (X - 18)^2)}$
:DrawF $14 - (3/5)\sqrt{(100 - (X - 20)^2)}$
:DrawF $10 - (1/2)\sqrt{(16 - (X - 20)^2)}$
:DrawF $14 + (1/2)\sqrt{(1 - (X - 27)^2)}$
:DrawF $14 + (1/2)\sqrt{(1 - (X - 13)^2)}$
:Shade $(12 - (3/4)\sqrt{(16 - (X - 20)^2)}, 14.5$
　$-(3/7)\sqrt{(49 - (X - 20)^2)})$

Casio fx-7700GE

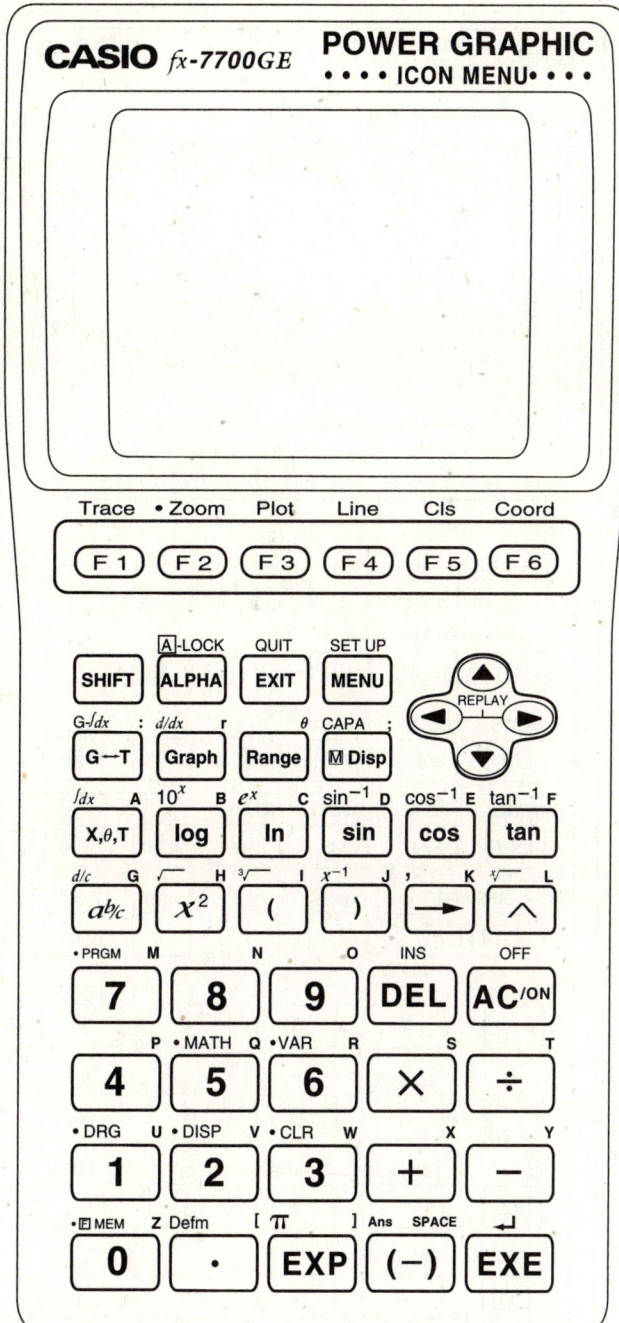

HP 38G

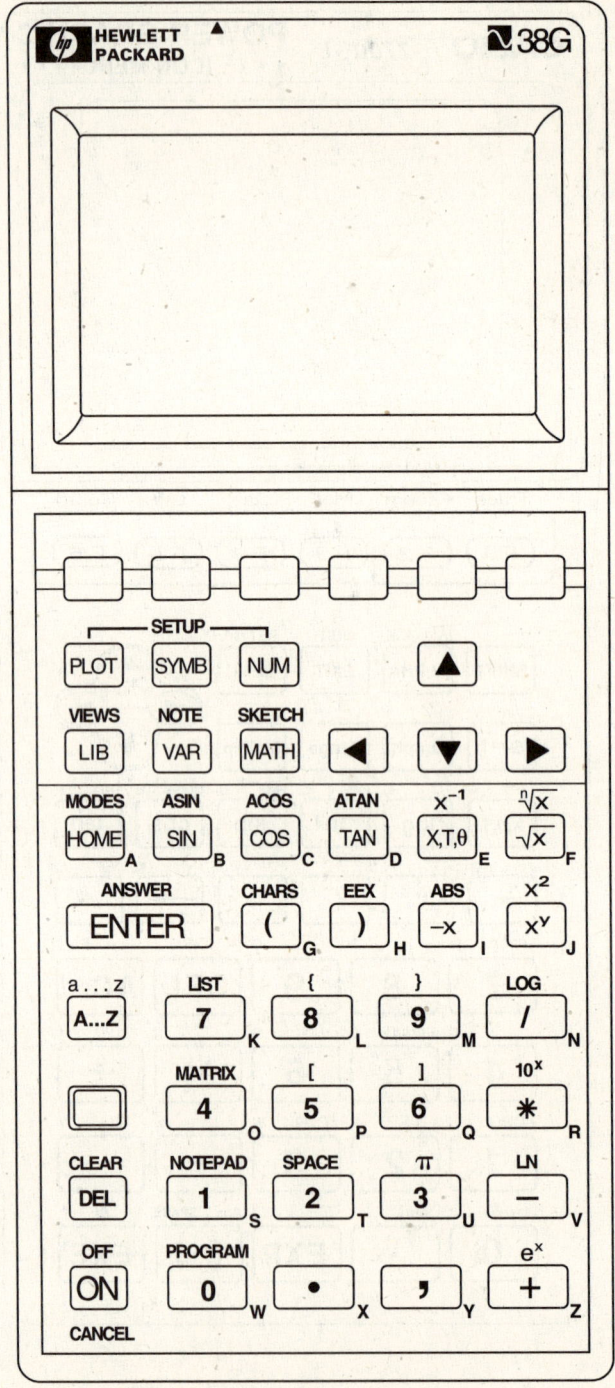

Sharp EL-9300C

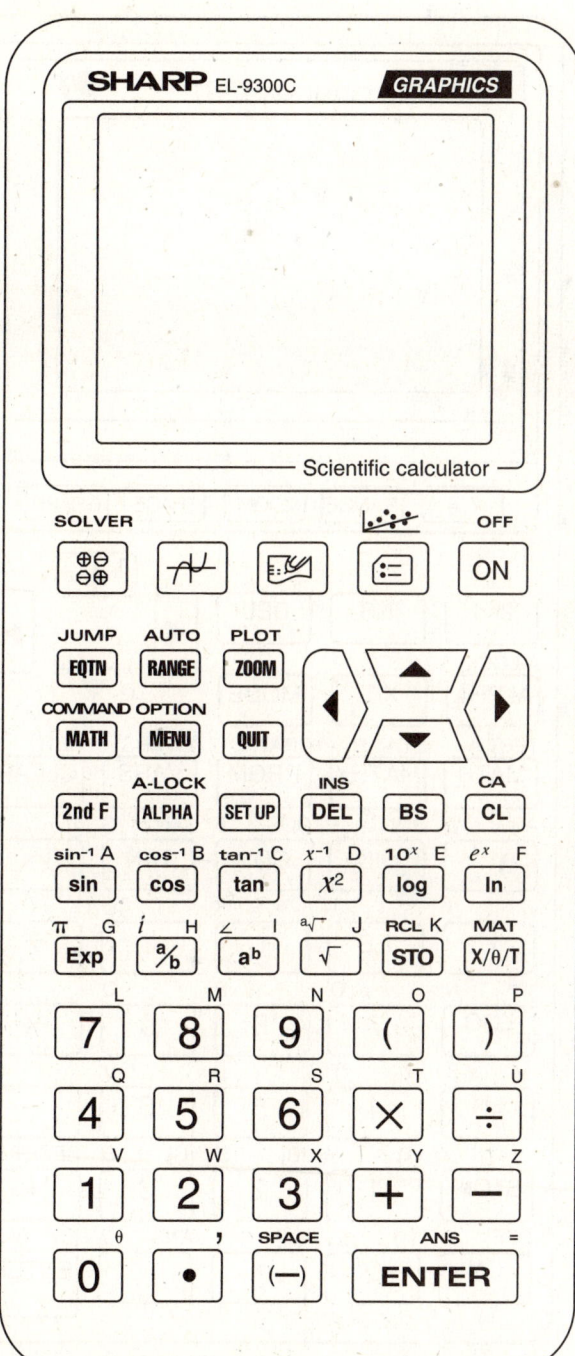

TI-81

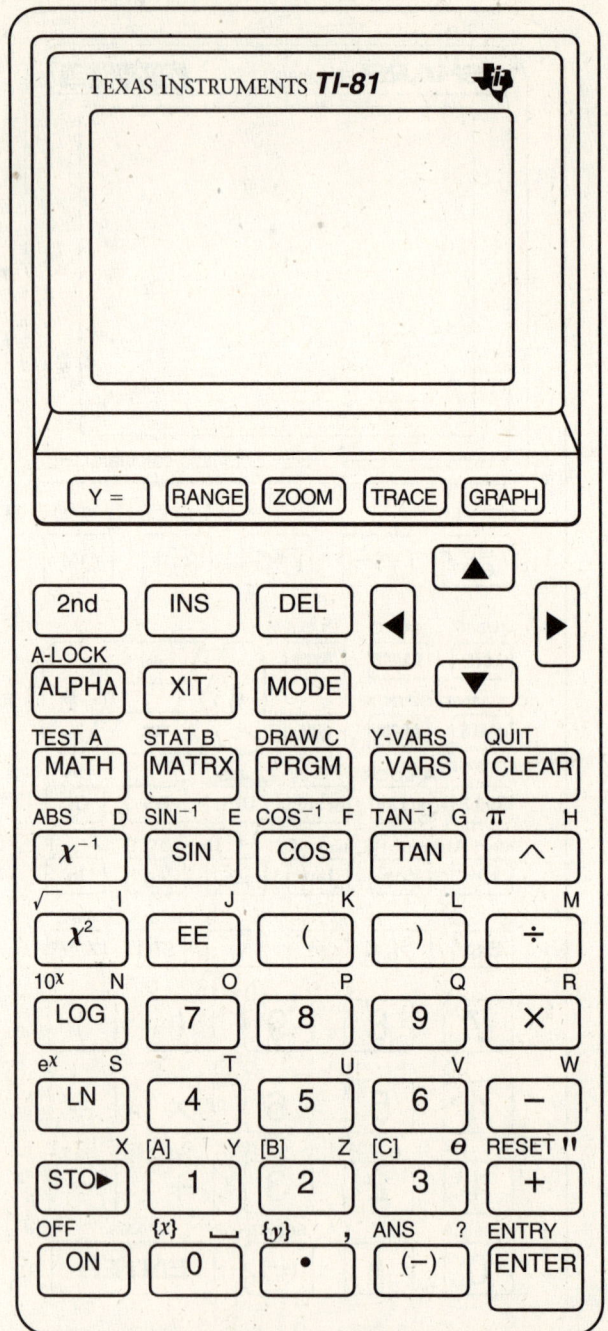

TI-82

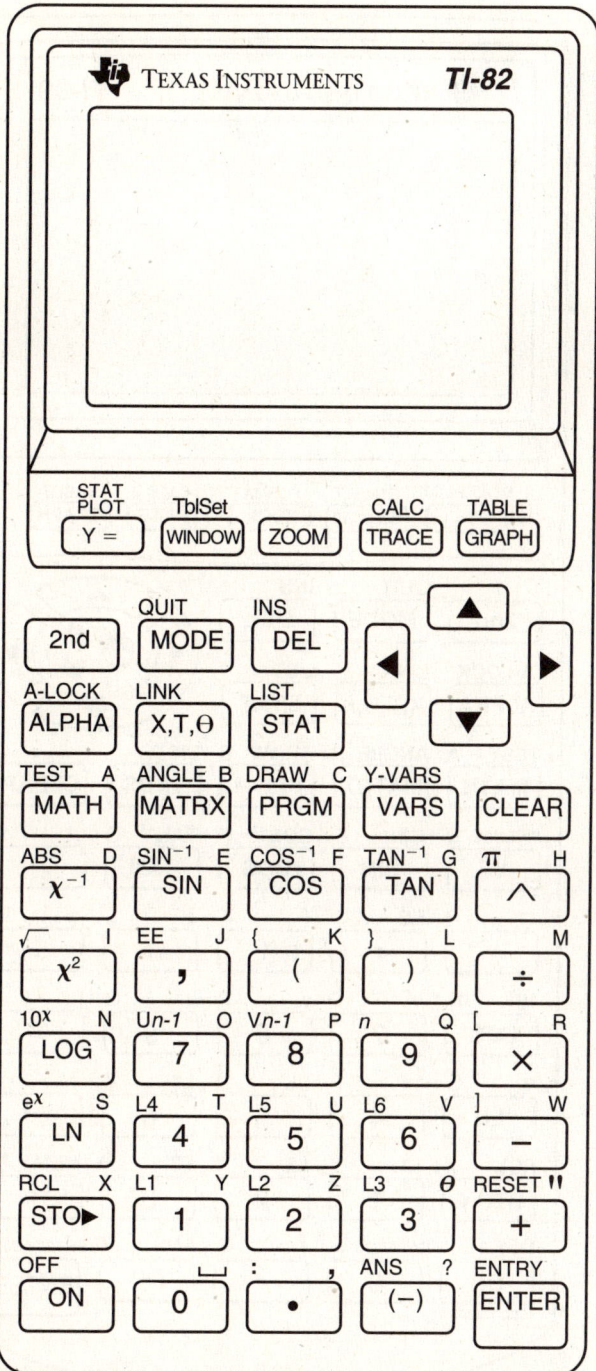

TI-83

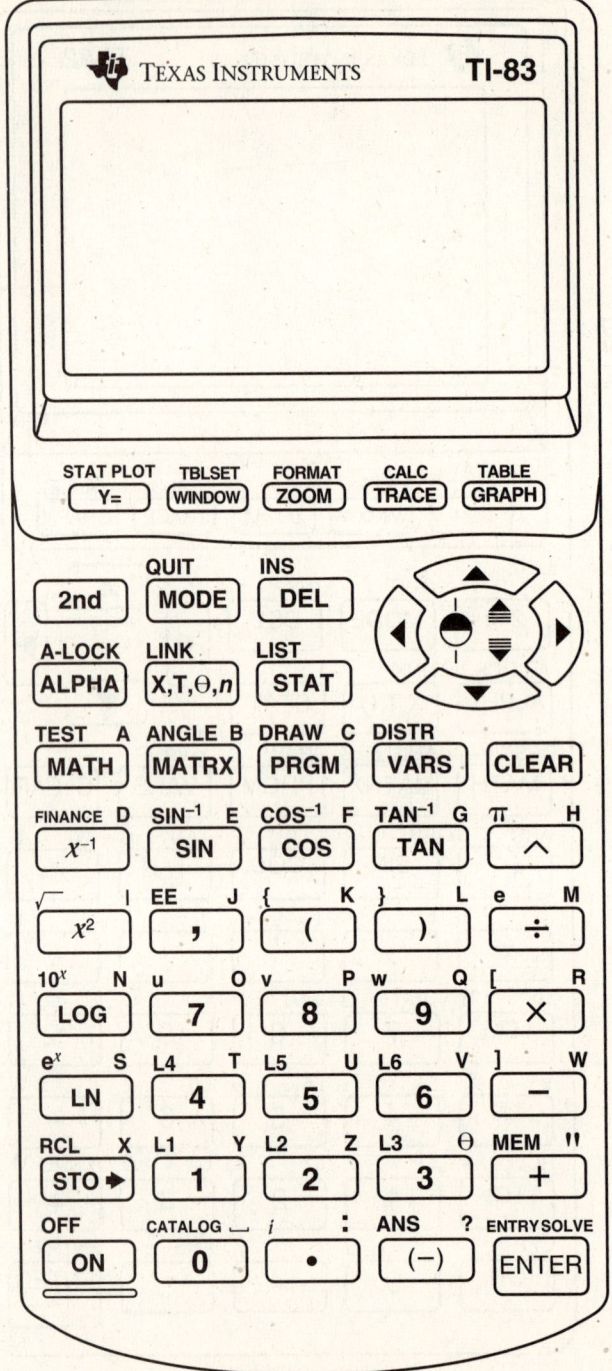

TI-92

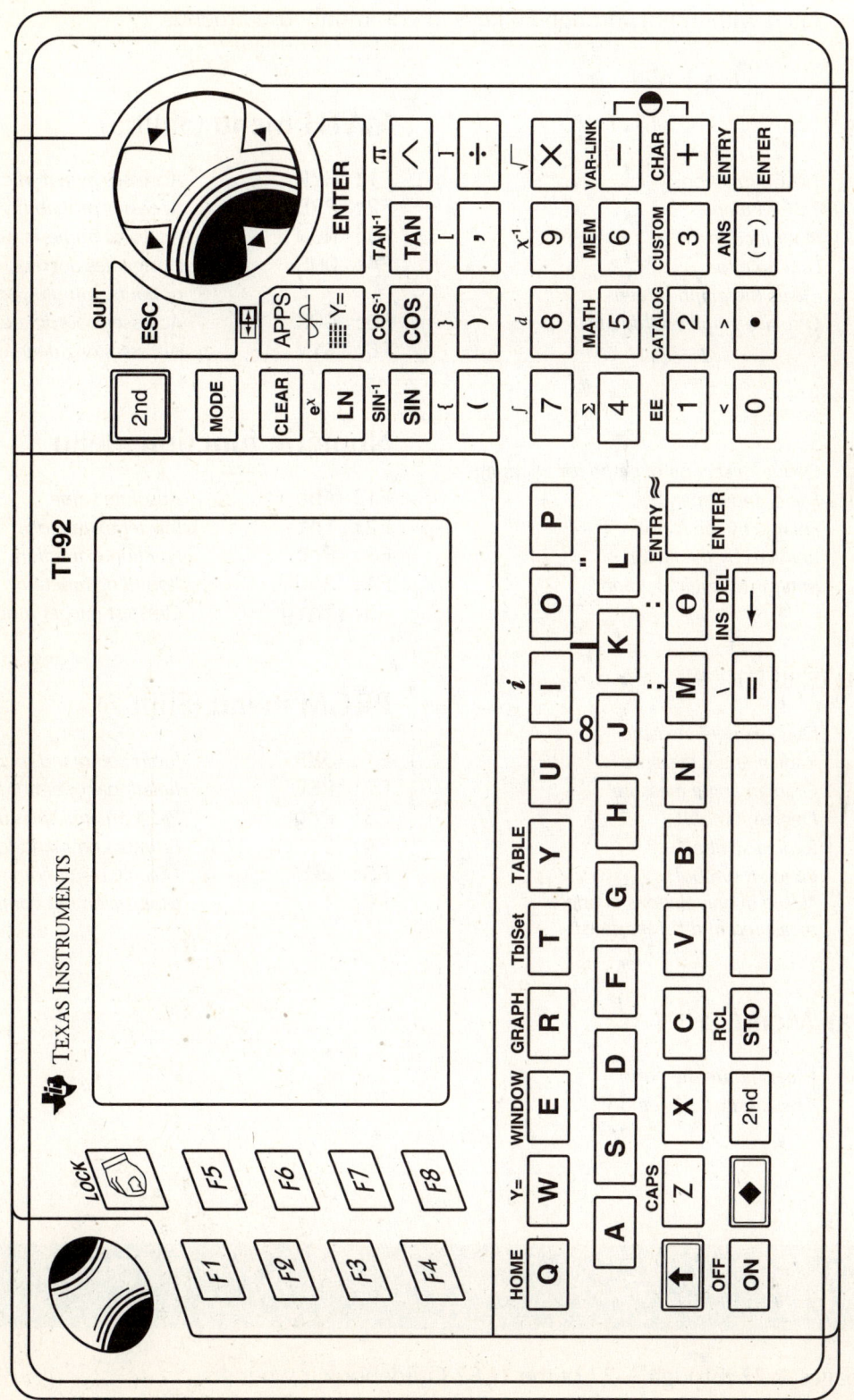

Menus: Casio fx-7700GE

There are numerous menus and submenus accessed by the F keys located on the first row of the Casio fx-7700GE calculator. The list below explains some of the abbreviations associated with the F1 through F6 keys in commonly used menus.

SHIFT menus

F1: TRC   TRACE function
F2: ZM   ZOOM menu
F3: PLT   Plot function
F4: LIN   Line function
F5: CLS   Clears the graph screen
F6: CRD   Displays graph coordinates

Zoom menu

F1: BOX   Defines a section of graph for zooming
F2: FCT   Factor input menu
F3: ×f   Enlarge by the factor
F4: ×1/f   Reduces by the factor
F5: ORG   Returns to original graph

Degree Menu (SHIFT 1)

F1: Deg   Degree angle measure
F2: Rad   Radian angle measure
F3: Gra   Gradian angle measure
F4: °   Degree symbol*
F5: r   Radian symbol*
F6: g   Gradian symbol*
    *Used in calculations of angles measured in different units.

Memory Clear Menu (SHIFT 3)

F1: Mcl   Clears entire memory
F2: Scl   Clears statistics memory

MATH menu (Shift 5)

F1: HYP   Accesses hyperbolic function menu
F2: PRB   Accesses probability function menu
F3: NUM   Accesses numeric function menu
F4: DMS   Designates degrees, minutes, seconds or hours, minutes, seconds
F5: COR   Accesses coordinate function menu
F6: SYM   Accesses engineering symbol menu

Numeric function menu

F1: Abs   Absolute value
F2: Int   Integer extraction
F3: Frc   Fraction extraction
F4: Rnd   Rounding function
F5: Intg   Greatest integer function

PRGM menu (Shift 7)

F1: JMP   Jump command menu
F2: REL   Relational operator menu
F3: Prg   Program area specification
F4: ?   Prompt command for input
F5: ◢   Display result command
F6: :   Multistatement connector

Menus: TI-82/83

Please refer to pages A-22 through A-27 of the TI-82 Guidebook (owner's manual) for a Menu Map. On these pages, you will find lists of the 72 menus available on a TI-82 graphing calculator. For the TI-83, see pages A-39 through A-48 of the manual.

Menus: TI-81

The TI-81 has 10 menus from which various functions can be selected. A menu may also contain other menus with additional functions. The lists below contain detailed information on the contents of six of the more commonly-used menus.

ZOOM Menu

1:	Box	Defines a section of graph for zooming
2:	Zoom In	Magnifies graph around the cursor
3:	Zoom Out	Views more of the graph around the cursor
4:	Set Factors	Changes Zoom-In, Zoom-Out factors
5:	Square	Sets equal-sized units on the X and Y axes
6:	Standard	Sets built-in default for RANGE values
7:	Trig	Sets built-in trig RANGE values.
8:	Integer	Sets integer values on the X and Y axes

MATRX menu (2 menus)

MATRIX EDIT

1:	RowSwap(	Swaps two rows
2:	Row+(	Adds two rows
3:	*Row(	Multiply row by number
4:	*Row+(	Multiply row, adds to another row
5:	det	Calculates determinant
6:	^{T}	Transposes matrix

MATRIX **EDIT**

1:	[A] 6×6	Edits matrix A
2:	[B] 6×6	Edits matrix B
3:	[C] 6×6	Edits matrix C

TEST Menu (SHIFT MATH)

1:	=	Equal to
2:	≠	Not equal to
3:	>	Greater than
4:	≥	Greater than or equal to
5:	<	Less than
6:	≤	Less than or equal to

PRGM Menu (3 menus)

EXEC EDIT ERASE		Executes selected program
EXEC **EDIT** ERASE		Edits selected program
EXEC EDIT **ERASE**		Erases selected program

MATH Menu (4 menus)

MATH NUM HYP PRB

1:	R▶P(	Rectangular to polar
2:	P▶R(	Polar to rectangular
3:	^{3}	Cubes a number
4:	$\sqrt[3]{\ }$	Finds cube root
5:	!	Factorial
6:	°	Degree notation
7:	r	Radian notation
8:	NDeriv(	Numerical derivative

MATH **NUM** HYP PRB

1:	Round(	Rounds a number
2:	IPart	Integer part of a number
3:	FPart	Decimal part of a number
4:	Int	Greatest integer function

MATH NUM **HYP** PRB

1:	sinh	hyperbolic sine
2:	cosh	hyperbolic cosine
3:	tanh	hyperbolic tangent
4:	sinh^{-1}	hyperbolic arcsine
5:	cosh^{-1}	hyperbolic arccosine
6:	tanh^{-1}	hyperbolic arctangent

MATH NUM HYP **PRB**

1:	Rand	Random number generator
2:	nPr	Number of permutations
3:	nCr	Number of combinations

STAT Menu (SHIFT MATRX) (3 menus)

CALC DRAW DATA

1:	1-Var	One-variable calculations
2:	LinReg	Linear regression
3:	LnReg	Logarithmic regression
4:	ExpReg	Exponential regression
5:	PwrReg	Power regression

CALC **DRAW** DATA

1.	Hist	Draws a histogram
2:	Scatter	Draws a scatter plot
3:	xyLine	Connects data points

CALC DRAW **DATA**

1:	Edit	Enters or edits data
2:	ClrStat	Clears data
3:	xSort	Orders data by X values
4:	ySort	Orders data by Y values

Index

ALPHA, 9
Arccos, Arcsin, Arctan, 31
asymptote, 25–26, 33, 43
BOX ZOOM, 17, 19
CALC menu, 34, 36, 40
Casio, 4, 7, 11–61, 73, 80
circle, 29, 66
CLEAR, 9, 48, 51, 53–54, 56–58
colon (:), 19, 23, 29
combinations, 60–61
complex numbers, (powers), 64
complete graph, 15, 20, 22, 27, 29
contrast, 8
cooperative groups, 5
correlation value, 55, 58–59
COS, 30, 41–42, 65
critical points of functions, 15, 22–23, 27, 39–40
curriculum, using the graphing calculator, 6
cursor, free–moving, 22, 24
curve fitting, 56–59
data, 48–50, 56
degrees, 13,30
DEL, 9, 11, 48
determinants, 46
discontinuity, 25–26
DRAW, 21, 23
editing, 9, 44, 48, 62
graphs, end behavior, 15, 27
ENTER/EXE, 9
exponential equations/functions, 32–33, 43, 54
expressions, 9, 11
factorial, 60–61
families of graphs, 37–38
fractions, 31, 61
functions, 14–20, 25–27, 30, 32–43, 54–59, 63, 68
   built–in, 30, 32
geometry, 65
   Hero's formula, 65
   Law of cosines, 65
histograms, 51–53
inequalities, 21, 22
INS, 11, 49, 62
inverses, 30, 47
iteration, 68
linear functions, 14–15, 34, 37, 63
lines of regression, 54–55
logarithms, natural and common, 32, 56–59

logarithmic functions/equations, 32, 33, 43
lower boundary, 21, 23, 40
Mandelbrot set, 68
matrices, 44–47
menu, 9–10, 12–14, 16–24, 28–31, 34, 36–37, 39, 47–50, 48–62, 76–77
mode, 12–13, 48, 51, 56–59
NCTM Standards, 5
ON/OFF, 8
parabola, 28, 38–39
permutation, 60
pi, 10, 31
probability, 60–61
programs, iv, 62–71
quadratic functions, 28, 64
radians, 13, 31
radical functions, 27
random numbers, 60, 62, 69
RANGE
   default, 13, 29
   setting, 13–14, 31
   squaring the screen, 29
   zoom, 16
rational functions, 25, 26
regression curves, 56
REPLAY, 5, 11
scale factor, 14
scatterplots, 54–55
second functions (2nd), 8–9
semicolon (;), 51–52
series, 67
SHADE, 21–23
SHIFT, 8
SIN, 30, 41–42
slope, 37, 56
solving equations, 34–36, 41, 43, 63, 64
square root key, 9, 28
squaring the screen, 29
standard viewing window, 13, 14
statistics, 48–59
   graphs, 50–53
   correlation value, 55, 58–59
   mean, median, 49–50
   standard deviation, 48–49
suppressing a graph, 37
systems
   functions, 19, 20, 34, 63
   inequalities, 23, 24

TAN, 30, 41, 42
templates, 73–79
   Casio fx–7700GE, 73
   HP–38–G, 74
   Sharp EL–4300C, 75
   TI–81, 76
   TI–82, 77
   TI–83, 78
   TI–92, 79
Texas Instruments, 4, 7, 10–71, 76–79
TRACE, 16–19, 22, 24–25, 34–36, 39–41, 43, 54, 55
trigonometric functions, 30, 41, 42
trigonometric identities, 42
trigonometric inverses, 30
upper boundary, 21, 23, 40
variables, 9
VARS, 56, 58, 59
vectors, (cross products, inner products), 66
vertex, 38
viewing window, 14
x-intercepts, 15, 21, 39, 41
y-intercepts, 15, 21, 37, 55
Y–VARS, 29
Y=, 14–45, 54–59
zeros, 35, 39–40
ZOOM, 10, 16–8, 24–25, 30, 34–36, 39–41, 45
   factors, 18–19